Mind Traps

and Breaking Free
through *God's Love*

by

JUDITH R. SHANNON

Judith R. Shannon

ISBN 978-1-64028-151-6 (Paperback)
ISBN 978-1-64028-152-3 (Digital)

Christian Faith Publishing, Inc.
296 Chestnut Street
Meadville, PA 16335
www.christianfaithpublishing.com

Judith Shannon, P. O. Box 3688
Mammoth Lakes, CA 93546
www.oneaccordministries.net

Printed in the United States of America

I dedicate this book with love to my friend Val.
I also dedicate this book to my loving husband, Dennis. His
viable suggestion to include a practical workbook format with
questions at the end of each section will prove to be of great value.

ACKNOWLEDGEMENTS

For several years, it has been my desire to put into book form the material I have been teaching and ministering to help identify and escape mind traps.

It is with heartfelt appreciation that I thank the many women in the Tuesday Morning Bible Group and those listed below for helping to bring this book to fruition.

Thank you to Irene Kish, for all the hours invested in transcribing and editing. Thank you to Julie and Patrick Castellana, Janice Henry and Michelle Rashid for their constructive comments after reading the manuscript.

Finally, and most especially, I want to thank my husband Dennis who believed in me and whose love and encouragement never wavered.

This book contains principles that work in overcoming mind traps. It is a working resource to help master tormenting thoughts, possess rest for your soul and live an overcoming life.

CONTENTS

SECTION I

INTRODUCTION TO MIND TRAPS

CHAPTER 1

You shall know the Truth...

Our communication system is based on words. We understand that words bring thoughts and thoughts bring images. When we hear the words, "A house with a red car in the driveway," those words form a thought and the thought forms a picture or image. The image could be either positive or negative. The image could bring the emotion of anger if the red car belongs to the demanding neighbor next door, or it could be the emotion of joy if the red car means our daughter is home for a visit.

Good images uplift our faith and bring liberty, while bad images contain bondage and oppression. Images that are according to the program of God and the Word of God bring life and peace, while images that are against God and His Word bring turmoil and death. They are not uplifting to our faith, and these negative images can start us down a destructive path that was either suggested by the devil, by others or ourselves.

For many years, I was taught by my own failures. Since 1976, I saw how idols gained entrance into my mind and formed my patterns of thinking. When the devil brought a suggestion to my mind and I took it as my own thinking, I went into a mind idolatry trap. If I did not recognize his deception, I was stalled for a time. Whether the devil instigated the trap or I fell into a trap of my own doing out of habit, the result was always the same. I eventually went from the mind trap into depression. Each time I traveled this route from trap to depression, I found God was with me and He always showed me the way out.

Over the years, I have isolated some mind idolatry traps in myself and in others. I recognized the same patterns of thinking that I had entertained in my friends, and the patterns all started with the same mind traps. I had to change my thinking patterns to become free of the mind traps. Many people who shared with me through counseling have realized the same freedom from mind traps.

When circumstances came into my life and I let them rule my emotions and actions, the same outcome surfaced regardless of whether the situations were less or more extreme. The outcome had a certain progression. I went from a mind trap to offense, then to rejection and finally into depression. Whenever I experienced a mind trap and this certain progression in my thinking, it left me an emotional wreck for a while. During these times, my life was a complete contradiction of what God, in His Word, said He wanted for my life.

Most of us blunder along blindly never really understanding why we are living defeated lives. We do eventually get back on the right track, but we need to see what caused us to derail in the first place to stop the cycle. The question I wanted to answer for myself was, "How do I get on track and stay there?" Consequently, I went on a quest to answer my question and achieve my goal. In an effort to live the victorious life that God's Word says we have in Christ, I began to trace each emotional disturbance in my life and founded upon something interesting. When I allowed destructive suggestions into my thoughts, I allowed my mind to trap me. Time and time again, I saw that these traps were a pattern of wrong thinking caused by a sense-ruled mind inspired by the devil!

In the last chapter of Ephesians, we are told to put on the whole armor of God to be able to stand against the wiles of the devil. In order to stand against something, we must have knowledge about it. We must know the source of it. This knowledge will equip us with the information we need to protect ourselves from being caught off guard. We need to realize there is a devil who is violently against us, and he wants us to believe his way of thinking. He tries to trick us into thinking that his thoughts are our thoughts, when he is the one who is actually speaking the suggestions to our minds. We have to recognize his wiles, his trickery and his schemes. He has a whole way of thinking that is contrary to the Word of God. I found a description of his thinking in James 3:14-16 (NKJ):

> *But if you have bitter envy and self-seeking in your hearts, do not boast and lie against the truth. This wisdom does not descend from above, but is earthly, sensual, and demonic. For where envy and self-seeking exist, confusion and every evil thing are there.*

When we are considering only ourselves and our own well-being, we are thinking contrary to God's way of thinking. Then our wisdom descends not from above, but is earthly, sensual and demonic. When envy and self-seeking are in our words, there is confusion and every evil work. This is when we become double minded. Being double minded means that we have one pattern of thinking in our heart and an opposite thinking in our minds. We are torn within ourselves with the conflict and start battling in our minds.

This kind of earthly, sensual and demonic thinking is common to man's way of thinking. It is based on our senses. It is made up of what we can see, hear, taste, smell and touch. The earthly circumstances we experience daily clamor for our attention. The words we hear fill our minds with thoughts and these go around and around in our minds as we dwell on them. This way of thinking is not Godly, but self-seeking. When we let envy and self-seeking rule within us, the result will be confusion and every evil work. These evil works, which are the wiles of the devil, will eventually wear us down and take over our thinking. We will become mentally weary and exhausted. This thinking is designed to defeat us.

It was because of these wiles of the devil that God gave us the Holy Spirit. With His help, some patterns of thinking can be defeated quickly. They are exposed in a flash of revelation! Others take longer. In some cases, there may be many layers of reasoning in our patterns of thinking, similar to an onion. We can peel them off a layer at a time or one section at a time, but by the time we find out our thinking, it may have already infiltrated into every area of our lives. This weakness always has some point of entrance. This entrance point was when we decided to take a thought, which created an image, and we formed a philosophy based on this image.

In my case, the idea of being unacceptable entered my mind in the third grade when the division tables were presented. This was when I checked out mentally. I could not learn the tables nor recite them orally when I was called on in front of the class. The Holy Spirit brought me all the way back to my third grade classroom and showed me this was where being unacceptable had its entry point in my life. Because I was publicly embarrassed and humiliated, I formed this negative self-image. At that time, I felt unacceptable to my peers and even to myself. I said, "I don't understand this and I can't do this!" So, I simply gave up!

Over the years, seeing myself as unacceptable became a recurring experience in my life because of this familiar pattern of thinking. I recognized this as a besetting sin as mentioned in Hebrews 12:1. A wile or scheme of the devil like this one usually has an early point of entry in childhood and is reinforced over and over again. Beset means "to attack from all sides, to besiege and harass."

When we were children someone may have said to us, "You are no good, and you will never amount to anything!" If statements like this are said to small children by verbally abusive parents, the children cannot combat this type of abuse. Children are vulnerable, and they believe what they hear and are affected by it. On the other hand, if we find ourselves, as adults, being talked to in this way, we must learn to reject this type of negative input. We must stop and protect ourselves by saying, "I cannot allow this person to be my only source of truth." We cannot embrace the statements of destructive people in our lives, because it is not what God says about us. More importantly, we must also catch our own negative thoughts about ourselves and start to reject them.

Because most children are not aware of the existence of the evil in the spirit world, they become easy prey to it. Because they do not know evil is against them, they can become easily influenced by the forces of darkness. Most parents are not aware of the spiritual warfare assigned to take over their children, so they do not pray to protect them from it.

When the Holy Spirit revealed the point of entry for being unacceptable, I began my journey of deliverance from it. Deliverance from a besetting sin pattern of thinking is possible, and it starts when something is revealed to us on the surface. By continually dealing with the revealed knowledge and combating the familiar pattern of thinking, the layers can be peeled off one by one. This is the way we move toward rightful thinking patterns—one layer at a time. In order to walk in freedom, we must understand the wiles that trapped us. They will be revealed to our spirit by the Holy Spirit and this revelation of the wile will enable us and keep us from this deception.

The Holy Spirit will continue to shine light on areas where the besetting sin pattern has been reinforced. He is so faithful in this. Once He has begun the good work in us, He will complete it. Sometimes, when the thinking comes to me and I do not discern the source of it, I still think of myself as being unacceptable. Other times, I catch it immediately. Sometimes I do, and sometimes I do not! But I am standing on the fact that by faith I am already delivered and established in the thought-life God wants me to have, and this thought-life is in line with His Word.

Let's look at what happened in the Garden of Eden. Eve was taken in by the lust of her eyes, the lust of her flesh and the pride of life, which is the spirit of the world. 1 John 2:15 talks about the spirit of the world:

> *Love not the world, neither the things that are in the world. If any man love the world, the love of the Father is not in him. For all that is in the world, the lust of the flesh, and the lust of the eyes, and the pride of life, is not of the Father, but is of the world.*

God gave Adam and Eve everything they needed in the garden, but He commanded them not to eat of the fruit of one tree. It was the tree of the knowledge of good and evil. Yet Eve was drawn away from obeying God's command by the spirit of the world. This was the devil. He lured her to look on the fruit and see its beauty. He lured her by the desire of her flesh and by making her think she would be like God, knowing both good and evil, if she ate the fruit. This was the pride of life. We allow ourselves to be lured by the devil when we give our minds over to contrary thinking.

When we choose contrary thinking, we become as Adam and Eve and move from a God-consciousness to self-consciousness. When we have self on the throne of our soul, our thinking is consumed with self-consciousness. Our self-image is threatened or enticed to greatness, and we become prime targets for the mind traps. Anytime we look at our circumstances or how a situation is affecting us, we move from God-consciousness, which is in our spirit, to self-consciousness which is in our soul. When we are self-ruled and not spirit-ruled, we render ourselves powerless. God cannot reach us in this position. God cannot give us His grace to deal with ourselves or the way we are thinking when we are ruled by self. When we take stock of our situation, we know that we have the provisions of God as our inheritance but they can only be appropriated when we are operating out of our spirit-man. We have to position ourselves in our spirit-man in order to receive God's grace and His way of thinking in our situation. We must switch to God's Word and hold onto what He has said in His Word instead of relying on and dwelling on our contrary thought patterns. Otherwise, we are still operating in our own mind control and self-will. We must move from self-consciousness to God-consciousness and from being self-ruled to God-ruled in order to tap into the grace of God found in His trusted words. We need to become established in God's way of thinking versus the world's way of thinking. Being out of the will of God costs each time because the price we pay when we line up with the devil's way of thinking is to fall into self-deception and bondage.

One of the verses that has helped me to check my thinking is found in Proverbs 3:5:

> *Trust in the Lord with all thine heart; and lean not unto thine own understanding. In all thy ways acknowledge him, and he shall direct thy paths.*

The understanding is part of the mind. In order to live in peace of mind, we must learn not to lean on our own understanding because our understanding, even after having a spiritual awakening, remains an enemy to God's way of thinking.

Another Scripture that helps my thinking is in Jonah 2:8: "They that observe lying vanities forsake their own mercy." I used this verse many times to get control over my mind because I got tired of forsaking my own mercy. I learned that God has mercy and grace for each one of us in our time of need, but I kept forsaking that mercy and grace because I observed circumstances.

If I listen to the devil, who is the father of lies, regarding the outcome of a circumstance, I would take on his lies as my truth. The devil's statements are always contrary to what God says in His Word. They would become lying vanities to me. These lying vanities are the things I assume from the words I hear all around me. The words I hear form my philosophies and the way I think about my world and myself, including my inner thoughts and the workings of my own mind.

My imagination also ran wild in assuming I could read other people's minds and know what they were thinking about me. My mind was always clanging, noisy and racing, making me an individual who rationalized, analyzed and speculated all the time. I worried about everything! If I could not find something to worry about, I invented something! This was my habitual pattern of thinking with no hope of changing, until my spirit was born of God.

The lying vanities were all contrary to Scripture so I had some fast decisions to make. I had to ask myself, "Is self on the throne in my thinking or have I made God the Lord of my thinking and the Lord of my life?" I turned and started to take what God said in His Word instead of continuing in my own wrong thinking. I said to my mind, "You will listen to the Word, accept and believe what it says, and receive it from the Father, in Jesus' Name!" This is the way I started controlling my mind. Instead of letting it harass me, I talked to my mind to get it under the control of my spirit. I literally had to tell my mind to shut up in Jesus' Name, and with the power of Jesus' Name, it would become quiet. Sometimes I was harassed with words and images fifty or sixty times a day! I had to speak to these words and images in order to gain control of my thinking. I practiced speaking Jesus' Name over and over again. I knew that with the authority of the spoken Word, the devil was defeated. This is how I developed a consciousness of God's authority in my life and my faith in the spoken Word, (Romans 12:1-3; Philippians 2).

When my spirit was regenerated, I was still the same in my soul for a time. I found out I was my own worst enemy! For example, in Al-Anon, a support group for families of alcoholics, I learned about "stinkin-thinkin". People with high imaginations play a lot of mind games and, in addition, are usually very emotional. I found out that my emotions were working against me most of the time, as well as my wrong-thinking patterns.

In Al-Anon, the most crucial thing I learned to do was to detach emotionally from the alcoholic family member I was obsessing over. This meant that I had to let the person I was emotionally enmeshed with be responsible for his own actions. His actions did not have to affect me. I had to give up my self-appointed role of being the caretaker for that person. I learned that everyone is responsible for what they say and do, no matter who they want to blame. If they said, "You got me into this mess," or "You made me act this way," I realized and recognized these types of statements were a cop-out on their part. The world system of thinking always points the finger of blame at the other person. I could not allow myself to be manipulated by them through false guilt and false responsibility.

On the other hand, if someone else's words or actions affected me, I came to realize that I allowed them to affect me. I had to take responsibility for what I decided to let affect me and not blame them for their words or actions. Each person is their own agent, and they alone are responsible for their own actions and reactions. When I realized this, self-discipline finally came into my life. I started practicing detaching emotionally, controlling my mind and my reactions to the things around me.

Because I was living with an alcoholic husband, I was dealing with a Jekyll and Hyde personality all the time. There was no consistency with him as far as our marriage relationship and our communication with each other were concerned. He had such erratic thinking that most of the time I did not know what the truth was! I made him the person I looked up to and depended upon for my identity, but he was not dependable. I could not have someone for my source of truth who was erratic and irresponsible himself! Yet, I looked to him for approval and acceptance but never received my expected response. I could not rely on his words. He did not know what the truth was for himself, so how could he show it to me? I was constantly double minded and confused.

When I started to look to God as my source, I learned to stop some of my irrational thinking. I had to learn to switch my reliance from my husband's words to God's Word. I could no longer have my source based on a person. I had to learn to rely on God.

In addition, I learned not to rely on my own way of thinking. At first, it was confusing because God was leading me in my spirit one way, while my mind was leading me in my old way of thinking. Slowly, I learned to sort out what the world system of thinking was, what my own mind was telling me and what God's thinking patterns were from His Word. I had to question the thoughts that I took automatically as truth and adjust my thinking to God's way of thinking.

At the same time, I was learning to detach emotionally. Whatever my husband said to me for a year and a half after we resumed our marriage, I could not take as truth. During that time, I had to rely on God's Word about my marriage. When it came to the success or failure of our marriage, I could not listen to my husband at all. If I went by where I thought he was mentally and emotionally, I was down in the pits! If I went by what he said, I was again down in the pits! I realized my emotions were going up or down based on my husband's input and his emotional temperature. He had a direct control over my mind and my emotions because he was still the center of my world and my source for truth.

My marriage and my husband were still my gods and I allowed him to have that power over me. He became the devil's advocate. He was the puppeteer and I was his puppet! Everything he said and did pulled my strings. I read in the Word that I was supposed to be more than a conqueror, but I realized that my life and my marriage at the time were not what the apostle Paul was talking about in Romans 8:37 when he said, "Nay, in all these things we are more than conquerors through him that loved us."

I began to realize the importance of submitting to the Word of God to get my mind controlled by my spirit. The person that I was in my spirit was the real person after God's own heart and my spirit was supposed to use my soul, not the other way around. We have had the order reversed since the fall of man. My soul is not to be generating of itself anymore, but it is to be under my spirit's control.

Romans 8:37 states we are to be more than conquerors. This became my goal, and I wanted to achieve it in my life. In Thayer's Lexicon it states, "To be more than a conqueror means to gain a surpassing victory." God's will for us is to live a life of surpassing victory all the time. God gave us a way on this earth to walk as Jesus would have walked. This does not mean we will not have problems, but we begin to rely on God's will for us to be victorious over all these problems. This is why in Philippians 4:11, Paul says, "For I have learned in whatsoever state I am therewith to be content." In the New International Version, this verse reads, "For I have learned to be content whatever the circumstance." Another Scripture is 1 Timothy 6:6 which reads, "But godliness with contentment is great gain."

So, whatever the circumstance, God wants us to find contentment. He wants us to learn to be emotionally detached from the people and circumstances in our lives that hinder us. When we become enmeshed emotionally in our circumstances and cannot break out of our old thinking patterns or the world's system of thinking, we are no good to Him or to ourselves. He wants us to be walking in surpassing victories all the time. This means to be at peace with our lives and dominate our circumstances because we have used the authority God has given us in His Word to appropriate the answers for all of our needs.

The more than conquerors verse in Romans 8:35-39 asks:

> *Who shall separate us from the love of Christ? Shall tribulation, or distress, or persecution, or famine, or nakedness, or peril, or sword? As it is written, for thy*

sake we are killed all the day long; we are accounted as sheep for the slaughter. Nay, in all these things we are more than conquerors through him that loved us. For I am persuaded, that neither death, nor life, nor angels, nor principalities, nor powers, nor things present, nor things to come, nor height, nor depth, nor any other creature, shall be able to separate us from the love of God, which is in Christ Jesus our Lord.

In Isaiah 26:3 (NIV) we read, *"You will keep him in perfect peace whose mind is steadfast, because he trusts in you."*

I knew I did not have peace in my mind. Every time I placed self on the throne of my thinking, I was operating from my soul and not from my spirit. If my mind had been occupied with Jesus and what He did for me, I would have had peace in my soul. If I had been relying on His love, I could have been more than a conqueror in my life. Because I was not operating in the love of God, my potential for being more than a conqueror and having peace was not realized at that time. I stood in my own way! I decided, since I could not trust myself or my husband for truth, I would take God's Word as truth in my life. I realized it did not matter what my husband said, but it did matter what God said about me and every situation I faced in my life.

God said in Ephesians 5:25 that my husband was to love me as Christ loved the Church. I started to believe this promise and to take Him at His Word. I received and started to practice a new pattern of thinking from God's Word. It included the thought from Proverbs that my husband was not taken by the flattery of a strange woman or by the batting of her eyelashes. I took these Scriptures to be my truth to hold me, no matter what I saw or heard in my natural circumstances.

What I was seeing and hearing at that time could have been a real threat to my thought-life and my peace of mind, but I stood against it. I had to stop my old habit of spiritualizing by reading meaning into every circumstance. I had to get my thought-life under control. My thought-life needed to be established in God's Word so

I could overcome the fear of other women and their influence on my husband. Somehow, I had to survive, and I could not look to my husband at this time for emotional nurturing and affirmation. He could not be my source for acceptance or approval anymore.

Other Scriptures such as Isaiah 55:6-9 (NIV) began to help my thinking:

> *Seek the Lord while he may be found; call on him while he is near. Let the wicked forsake his way and the evil man his thoughts. Let him turn to the Lord, and he will have mercy on him; and to our God, for he will freely pardon. For my thoughts are not your thoughts, neither are your ways my ways, declares the Lord. As the heavens are higher than the earth, so are my ways higher than your ways, and my thoughts than your thoughts.*

Isaiah said God's thoughts are not our thoughts, and His ways are not our ways. God's thoughts are higher than our thoughts, and His ways are higher than our ways. We must learn a new way of thinking. We can ask the Holy Spirit to show us what Jesus' reaction would be in the situation we are facing. We must ask ourselves, "What would Jesus do in this situation?" And let the Holy Spirit guide us. Even though my thoughts and ways are not like God's thoughts and ways, I can rely on the Holy Spirit to teach me to think in new ways. For myself, I knew there must be a positive, faith-building way of thinking as a child of God. With practice, I finally came to a place in my life where I preferred my thinking to be. Now my thinking, with the help of the Holy Spirit, has given my mind rest and peace and I am experiencing what is described in 1 Corinthians 2:9 (NIV):

> *No eye has seen, nor ear has heard, no mind has conceived what God has prepared for those who love him but God has revealed it to us by his Spirit.*

We can, with the Holy Spirit's help, know how God thinks about us and we can have His thoughts going through our minds. Since we have the Holy Spirit living inside of us and He is called the Spirit of Truth, it is His ministry to reveal truth to us. We are to ask Him what the truth is in every situation.

In John 16:13-15 we see the relationship we are to have with the Holy Spirit:

> *Howbeit when he, the spirit of truth, is come, he will guide you into all truth: for he shall not speak of himself; but whatsoever he shall hear, that shall he speak: and he will show you things to come. He shall glorify me: for he shall receive of mine, and shall show it unto you. All things that the Father hath are mine: therefore, said I, that he shall take of mine, and shall show it unto you.*

When I found this Scripture, I stayed on it and meditated on it in my mind. I literally parked myself on this Scripture! I expected the Holy Spirit to be truth to me, just as the Word said. The verse said He is the Spirit of Truth within me and it is part of His ministry to show me the truth in every situation. I needed truth in my life in a big way! This verse also said, "He will show me things to come." I could be prepared before they appeared in the natural. This Scripture had a calming effect on my clanging and noisy mind.

It gave me tremendous peace of mind to know that the Holy Spirit would help me and I would no longer be caught off-guard and left to my own reactions and resources. In every situation, I consulted with the Holy Spirit and asked Him to show me the truth. If I had peace in my heart, I would believe I was in God's will. If I did not have any direction, I would ask and receive revelation knowledge on the situation and wait for peace in my heart. I did not move just because all the outside circumstances lined up, unless they confirmed what was already in my heart.

In the beginning, I asked for two or three confirmations to what I believed was the will of God. I grew in assurance over time. I would recognize the confirmations and be able to step out in faith and have peace. A time came when I did not need confirmations anymore but had grown accustomed to His voice and confident in His directions. We are to have a confidence in what the Holy Spirit has started He will perform until the day of Christ Jesus. We are being conformed to the image of Jesus. Our responsibility is to yield to the Holy Spirit as soon as we know His will and react as Jesus would react to every situation.

In the upcoming chapters of Section One, we will be looking at the soul of man, what role renewing the mind plays, how words create thoughts and thoughts create images and how each mind trap is opposite to the characteristics of the love of God.

In Section Two, the mind traps will be explained. They will be presented in the order I recognized and learned them from the Holy Spirit, along with personal and Biblical examples.

Section Three shows the reactions to the mind traps and how to stop them from becoming more of a stronghold in our lives.

Section Four reveals the recovery process from mind traps and how to maintain the freedom Jesus gave us.

And the very God of peace sanctify you wholly: and I pray God your whole spirit and soul and body be preserved blameless unto the coming of our Lord Jesus Christ.

—1 Thessalonians 5:23 (KJV)

Our mind is the battleground and the arena where we fight our battles. The mind is the part of the soul that is like a computer that stores knowledge from both the spiritual and natural realms. Jesus said in John 6:63, "*The words that I speak unto you, they are spirit and they are life.*" From this Scripture, we know that words are spiritual and established in the spirit realm. Words are the way images are transmitted when the words are understood by the mind. Jesus' words transmit life to us because they contain spiritual forces that create images of life. On the negative side, since words are spiritual and established in the spirit realm, they can also create negative images of fear, anger, jealousy, and death. Whose words are we listening to—Jesus' words or the devil's words? Do we have faith-filled thoughts or fear-filled thoughts? Just because we cannot see into the spiritual realm does not mean this realm does not exist and the inhabitants of this realm are not trying to talk to us.

Physicists have documented that there are ten dimensions to the spirit realm, but man has experienced only three dimensions so far. The principalities and powers that are against us are constantly trying to attack our minds with suggestions. Since the mind of man is neutral and will transmit whatever input it hears or receives, we pick up these thoughts and images as our own, not knowing their subtle origin. When we take in thoughts and images that are contrary to God, we experience the conflict between our soul and our spirit. The battle will be in our mind. We get into these battles because we do not rule over our minds.

Third John 2 says, *"Beloved, I wish above all things that you prosper and be in health as your soul prospers."* John, under the inspiration and guidance of the Holy Spirit, is saying in this passage that he is praying above everything else in life that we may experience health, physical healing, and material prosperity or material success in this life depending on the condition of our soul. Is our soul succeeding in life? The soul is made up of the mind governing the intellect, the will, and the emotions of man. We need to ask ourselves if we are maintaining a healthy soul life.

The battle we face in our soul is focused primarily in the area of our mind. When we think about a negative situation or a possible disaster happening to us, our emotions get involved. If we let our emotions run rampant, they will interfere with our peace of mind. We can learn to control our emotions by our will, but since controlling them does not come naturally to us, we will have to practice. Practicing will establish them into our thinking patterns, but it will take some time and effort. Some have not gained mastery over their emotions because they have not put in the time and effort it takes to do so. Romans 8:3–6 gives us these instructions:

> *For what the law could not do, in that it was weak through the flesh, God sending his own Son in the likeness of sinful flesh, and for sin, condemned sin in the flesh: That the righteousness of the law might be fulfilled in us, who walk not after the flesh, but after the Spirit. For they that are after the flesh do*

mind the things of the flesh; but they that are after the Spirit, the things of the Spirit. For to be carnally minded is death; but to be spiritually minded is life and peace.

So where are we then? Are we in Christ Jesus? Are we spiritually in Him, and are we also mentally in Him? As we said before, if we are mentally in Him, we are not going to mind the things of the flesh and walk after the flesh. We are not going to let our carnal, sense-ruled mind have the last word in our thinking and in our actions. We will live by what God says in His Word instead of by what our sense-ruled mind says to us. If we want to live by the authority of God's Word, we cannot walk after the flesh or what comes in through our senses, but we must walk after the spirit. Romans 8:2 says, "*For the law of the spirit of life in Christ Jesus has made me free from the law of sin and death.*" We find true freedom and prosperity for our soul when we walk in our spirit.

The Mosaic Law could not bring righteousness to man since no one could fulfill the whole law and accomplish salvation as Christ did for us. God dealt with the flesh of man under the Old Covenant, but under the New Covenant He deals with the spirit of man. He deals with our spirit, the part of our being over which the spiritual laws have authority and jurisdiction. The way to experience soul prosperity and physical health is to walk in our spirit where we can experience the spiritual principles of God. When we keep our souls in submission to the authority of God, our souls will prosper.

While we are in this life, we all live in a flesh suit but we do not have to mind the things of the flesh as our only source of truth. We want life and peace for our souls. In order to get that life and peace, we have to make the choice to live after the spirit. If we stay in our sense-ruled mentality, it will bring death to our thinking. It is an enemy because it is hostile to God's way of thinking. It is also hostile to our spirit-man way of thinking. When we are operating from our spirit-man, it brings us life and peace, while the flesh-man brings us death every time. We are to reign in life by the choices we make and not let our circumstances reign over us. We have a choice about what we think. We do not have to be victims of our own negative thinking patterns.

When we came to Christ, no matter how old we were, we were ruled by the input from our senses. This was the basis for all our knowledge up until the time we accepted Christ into our hearts. So, the question is, "Are we going to continue our natural kind of thinking, even after our spirit comes alive to God?" Yes, we most certainly will for a time, until we realize that our soul is hostile to the principles of God. Our soul is the area that we are responsible for changing— from thinking according to the world's system to thinking according to God's thinking found in His Word.

1. Where is the battleground?

   _____

2. What did Paul pray for us to be?

   _____

3. How is man put together?

   _____

4. What do we have to do with our soul?

   _____

CHAPTER 3

Renewing the Mind

We are commanded to renew our minds in God's Word, but it is much easier for us to go along with our old familiar thinking patterns. Our mind will not of itself choose renewing. God has bought our spirit and our body, but not our soul. Our soul is our responsibility. It is up to us to renew our mind, which is part of our soul. Romans 12:1–3 (NIV) tells us:

> *Therefore, I urge you, brothers, in view of God's mercy, to offer your bodies as living sacrifices, holy and pleasing to God—this is your spiritual act of worship. Do not conform any longer to the pattern of this world, but be transformed by the renewing of your mind. Then you will be able to test and approve what God's will is—his good, pleasing and perfect will.*

We choose to give our bodies to God, to be used by Him. We choose to allow His presence and His abilities to flow through us to other people. Even though we are walking in this world, Scripture says we must not conform to its system of thinking. We must choose to change our thinking and thereby become transformed by the renewing of our minds.

A corresponding Scripture that says our bodies and spirits belong to God is found in 1 Corinthians 6:19–20:

> *What? Know ye not that your body is the temple of the Holy Ghost which is in you, which ye have of God, and ye are not your own? For ye are bought with a price: therefore, glorify God in your body, and in your spirit, which are God's.*

Our bodies and spirits belong to God, but our soul can be influenced by the devil. This is the place he constantly brings suggestions to us for action. I have said to myself, "Lord, I yield my mouth, I yield my ears, I yield my hands to you, because I desire to bring Your life and Your love to people. I am going to cooperate with You because I don't want to conform myself to this world's system of thinking. I want to be transformed by the renewing of my mind. I am going to be diligent to read Your Word, and it will renew my mind. Your Word is going to wash my mind with words of life."

John 15:3 says, "Now you are clean by the words which I have spoken to you." This is called the washing of the Word. The Word cleanses our soul. After a steady diet of the Word, good teaching, good fellowship, and choosing to separate from the world's system of thinking, our mind will stay in submission to our spirit.

Another critical part of renewing our mind is not to be passive in a system of thinking that is against God. We cannot be conformed to this world's thinking and still fully serve God. We cannot be in both places. There is no such thing as deciding to live by the Word of God as our final authority and then being passive to the influence of the world's thinking on our soul. We cannot operate successfully as a spiritual person and still stay in the passive mode. When a person is coasting through life, they are actually going downhill. We must be proactively engaged.

The Bible tells us we are to be the head and not the tail. We do not want to be in the tail position—being defensive. We need to be in the head position and take an active offensive stand. To be *more than a conqueror* means to occupy until Christ comes back. This *occupying* means working out the authority God gave us over our soul. It means to practice getting our soul under the authority of God.

God tells us in His Word that we can have victory in every situation (see 2 Corinthians 2:14). If this is so, then why are so many Christians living an emotional roller-coaster existence? Why are they up one week and down the next? In my experience, I found the key to having an established soul is having a controlled pattern of thinking. To have this, we must put our mind in a place of neutrality. We cannot allow our mind to form an image or picture on any desired outcome with the hidden motive to further *self* because if we do, we will fall into the expectation mind trap (to be discussed fully in the "Expectation" chapter in Section II).

Our mind is in the habit of forming images for every suggestion that comes to it. When we allow an expectation to be in the center of our thinking, we get excited over the situation and invest emotional energy into a preconceived outcome. We expend this energy when we picture how we want it to turn out. We would be better off not allowing our mind to picture anything at all. This is what I mean by keeping the mind in a place of neutrality. The reason to keep our mind in neutral is to avoid the mind trap of expectation. If the event does not turn out the way we expected it to or the person does not say or do what we expected them to say or do, we become angry, which is the expression of offense. We can then become disappointed in others and even ourselves for getting angry and then fall into depression. This emotional roller-coaster ride is what we can avoid by keeping our mind in neutral.

The only thing we should let our mind picture is our spiritual, physical, mental, emotional, financial, and social needs being met by God, His Word, and the Holy Spirit. We need to roll the care of every situation over onto God and let Him carry the weight of the outcome (Philippians 4:6; Proverbs 16:3, AMPC). This is the way to avoid falling into disappointment and even depression if the situation does not turn out the way we expected it to turn out. Instead, receive from Him a peaceful mind in all our situations, in Jesus' Name.

There is a story about a monkey who put his hand into a food jar. He grabbed some food but when he tried to pull his clenched food-filled fist out, the jar opening was not wide enough. He could take his hand out only if he opened his fist and let go of the food. When the storekeeper found him, he still had his hand in the jar and he got caught! We need to not let the devil catch us holding onto things that have become our masters. Whatever we cannot let go of on this earth has us in bondage. Our way for victory in this life has already been provided, but in order to walk in that victory, we must dethrone *self* and put God on the throne of our soul and keep Him there. Then everything else will assume its proper place and perspective in our lives (Matthew 6:33).

Putting the Word of God into our thoughts instead of thinking about the circumstances is how renewing the mind works. It is the practice of taking the Word as our truth to hold our mind instead of dwelling on the details of our negative situations. So to be transformed by the renewing of our mind is possible, and it is also possible to get out of this world's system of thinking. It is done by renewing our mind with the Word of God. The benefit of renewing our minds is so that we can scrutinize for ourselves and prove what is the good, acceptable, and perfect will of God for our lives.

Since we have been born again and renewed by the Spirit, we are to identify with Christ and remember who we have been made in Christ. These things must be preeminent in our thinking. When we have been trapped or when we have the potential to be trapped, it helps us to understand what we are dealing with spiritually. When we understand what we are dealing with, we can aim at getting out instead of getting frustrated and giving up. It also helps to know that there is a way out (1 Corinthians 10:13). People make the statement, "You know very well they can't change. They will never change!" This lie is from the devil! We have Jesus Christ as our self-identification. When we identify with Him and become an imitator of Him, we can change anything. Change comes as a result of a decision of our will, and it is realized because of God's love for us. We may not think we are strong enough to change, but we can change our reality or experience because of God's love and His promises in His Word. What is impossible with men is possible with God (Matthew 19:26).

1. How can we change our thinking patterns?

   _____

2. Why do we need to renew our minds?

   _____

3. Why should we take an active approach to God's Word?

   _____

4. How do we get into a head position with the devil?

   _____

5. How can a Christian be up one day and down the next?

   _____

6. What does it mean to have your mind in a neutral position?

   _____

7. What kind of a mental picture should a believer take?

   _____

8. What is the importance of the monkey holding on to the food?

_____

9. Is there a way out of a situation for a believer?

_____

CHAPTER 4

Idolatry

And what agreement hath the temple of God with idols? For ye are the temple of the living God: as God hath said I will dwell in them and walk in them; and I will be their God, and they shall be my people.

—2 Corinthians 6:16 (KJV)

Wherefore, my dearly beloved, flee from idolatry.

—1 Corinthians 10:14 (KJV)

Finally, my brethren, be strong in the Lord and in the power of his might. Put on the whole armor of God that ye may be able to stand against the wiles of the devil. For we wrestle not against flesh and blood, but against principalities, against powers, against the rulers of the darkness of this world, against spiritual wickedness in high places. Wherefore, take unto you the whole armor of God, that ye may be able to withstand in the evil day, and having done all, to stand. Stand therefore, having your loins girt about with truth, and having on the breastplate of righ-

*teousness; And your feet shod with the preparation
of the gospel of peace: Above all, taking the shield of
faith, wherewith ye shall be able to quench all the
fiery darts of the wicked. And take the helmet of
salvation, and the sword of the Spirit, which is the
word of God: Praying always with all prayer and
supplication in the Spirit and watching thereunto
with all perseverance and supplication for all saints;
And for me, that utterance may be given unto me,
that I may open my mouth boldly, to make known
the mystery of the gospel, for which I am an ambas-
sador in bonds: that therein I may speak boldly as I
ought to speak.*

—Ephesians 6:10–20 (KJV)

The Old Testament gives us many examples of idolatry. One of the clearest accounts is found in 2 Chronicles 33:1–17:

*Manasseh was twelve years old when he began to
reign and he reigned fifty and five years in Jerusalem
and did that which was evil in the sight of the Lord
like unto the abominations of the heathen whom the
Lord had cast out before the children of Israel.*

Manasseh put up altars to Balaam and built again the high places that his father Hezekiah had torn down. And he made groves and worshiped all the hosts of heaven and served them. He also built altars in the house of the Lord where the Lord had said, "*In Jerusalem shall my name be forever.*" He built altars for worshiping angels, the hosts of heaven in the two courts of the temple. And he made his children walk through fire in the valley of the son of Benhinnom. He observed times, consulted horoscopes, and used enchantments. He practiced witchcraft, sorcery, and communicated with familiar spirits, spiritists, and wizards.

This passage says that Manasseh "wrought much evil in the sight of the Lord to provoke him to anger." He even set an idol or carved image in the house of God. God said to David and to Solomon, his son, "In the house and in Jerusalem, which I have chosen before all the tribes of Israel, will I put my name forever." God promised never to remove Israel from the land, but His promise had a condition. The people must take heed and do all God had commanded them to do. He was referring to the Ten Commandments, "According to the whole law and statutes and ordinances by the hand of Moses."

Manasseh brought the nation of Israel into idolatry. "So Manasseh made Judah and the inhabitants of Jerusalem to err and to do worse than the heathen . . ." The Lord spoke to Manasseh and to the people, but they would not listen to Him. So the Lord brought the armies of the king of Assyria down upon Manasseh, and they carried him away into captivity to Babylon.

But Manassah came back to God as it says in 2 Chronicles 33:12:

> *And when he was in affliction, he besought the Lord God of his fathers, And he prayed unto him: And he was entreated of him, and heard his supplications, and brought him again unto Jerusalem into his kingdom.*

It goes on to say that, "Then Manasseh knew that the Lord he was God." In his affliction, Manasseh turned to God and repented. He began to do good works for the fortification of the city walls. He built the outer walls of the City of David, and he provided captains of war for all the fenced cities of Judah. We see in 2 Chronicles 33:15, "*And he took away the strange gods and the idols out of the house of the Lord and in Jerusalem and cast them out of the city.*" He also repaired the altar of the Lord in the temple and sacrificed peace offerings and thank offerings to God. He commanded Judah to serve the Lord God of Israel, and the people sacrificed and worshiped God again in the high places.

Manasseh was not the only king to do evil in the sight of God, but his example of falling into idolatry is one of the most serious since he even put a carved idol in the temple. When evil was fulfilled and reached a certain point in Manasseh's life, it gave access to the devil to bring the curses. In this passage, we also see the faithfulness of God who heard Manasseh when he was in his affliction and restored him.

All the cursing and blessing here on earth are set up in the spirit realm. When cursing catches us, we reap its consequences! Sin clicks into whatever is already set up in the spiritual realm to be the corresponding curse for that sin. In the same way, our blessings catch up with us and we reap more blessings. When we are doing the right things in God and are obeying Him, we will reach a point when the blessings will come upon us and overtake us. They will come from the spiritual realm to the natural realm and actually manifest themselves in our lives. These blessings are a result of our obedience to the things that He has instructed us to do, and the things that we have done out of our love for God.

Psalm 106:13–48 gives us an account of Israel's idolatry and the price they had to pay for it. In verse 21 it says, "*They forgot God their Savior.*" They forgot where they came from and who brought them out of the bondage of slavery in Egypt. They forgot all their former blessings and that God was the great *I AM* to them.

In verse 36 it says, "*And they served their idols: which were a snare unto them.*" There is an entrapment that comes upon us when we are serving idols. I remember when my emotional life was a trap to me. I felt like I was walking around with a silver ring in my nose. In ancient times, the household slaves had silver rings in their nostrils. They could be confined or chained to the wall by them or dragged around. I felt like I was being pulled here and there, back and forth, by the ring that the devil had put in my life. When I was serving idols, the devil deceived me into thinking and doing whatever he wanted me to do.

In verse 39 we read, "*Thus were they defiled with their own works and went a whoring with their own inventions.*" Verse 42 says, "*Their enemies also oppressed them and they were brought into subjection under their hand.*" Based on these verses and countless other examples in the Old Testament, we see that there is a price we pay for idolatry. The people of the Old Testament made graven images and worshiped other gods instead of the one true God, Jehovah. We in turn, allow images in our minds to become our idols. We must take these images or high things that exalt themselves against the knowledge of Christ and capture every thought and every wrong pattern of thinking (2 Corinthians 10:3–6). In order for God to say we were to capture every thought, this must be possible or He would be unjust. All His callings come with His equipping in Christ.

Idolatry is not without a cost. When we are serving idols, we forget who God is to us. We become entrapped. We become ensnared. We become defiled. We go off in our own way and in our own high-mindedness. We become a slave to the devil which is the world's way of thinking. We come under whatever lords it over us, and idolatry can really lord it over us! We think we are free to serve our own gains, but we become just another victim of the devil's oppression. These are strong words, but this is exactly what happens when we fall into idolatry.

Second Corinthians 6:16 says:

> *What agreement hath the temple of God with idols?*
> *For ye are the temple of the living God; as God hath*
> *said, I will dwell in them and walk in them; and I*
> *will be their God and they shall be my people.*

We can have this experience today, and God desires us to have it. We have our shepherd with us now, caring for each of us as one in His flock. We are His temple. He wants to dwell in us and be our God, and He wants us to be His people.

First Corinthians 10:14 says, "*Wherefore my dearly beloved, flee from idolatry.*"

Some people think idol worship was practiced in ancient times, in the Old Testament or in primitive cultures. But this Scripture from Corinthians is taken from the New Testament, which means that there must be idols in our lives today. We do have many idols that we worship. Some worship the idol of entertainment and sit glued to their TV sets. There are material idols, people idols, knowledge idols, and money idols. The biggest idol is the idol of *self.* We all have a strong drive for self-fulfillment and to do it in our own strength. This is what makes the *self* our strongest idol. We must deal with, flee from, and overcome the pull of *self* by keeping it dead (separated from influence on ourselves and our life). We must do whatever it takes to be free from the idol of *self*.

Since we are the temple of God (1 Corinthians 3:16–17) and He is residing within us, when we go into idolatry we become divided between what the *self* wants to do and what our *spirit-man* knows to do. It becomes a power play between the two of them. The Bible asks us, *"What agreement hath the temple of God with idols?"* There is no agreement. We choose by our own will to go into idolatry. And our spirit-man has to let us go because the *self* has made that decision. God made us free moral agents, and He will not force His will on us. We can either go to the spiritual information in our thinking or learn from God's Word how we are to think, speak, and act, or we can choose *self* and go into idolatry and bondage.

In Galatians 5:20, idolatry is the fifth in a long list of the works of the flesh and comes after adultery, fornication, uncleanness, and lasciviousness. Yet, most of the time we do not realize we are walking in the flesh if we do not take control of and rule over our thinking. It catches us off guard. This is why we get entrapped and why idolatry becomes so oppressive to our spirit and to our lives.

In Ephesians 6:11–20, we are advised to put on the whole armor of God. We make the decision to put on the whole armor. We must have a constant consciousness of the armor in place, protecting us. We receive it as part of our lives and walk in it. It is just like the grace of God. Once we have it, it stays with us. It does not leave us. We can have different degrees of grace, but it is always there.

The whole armor is to enable us to be strong in the Lord and able to stand firm against the *wiles* of the devil. According to the dictionary, *wiles* are "sly schemes, conniving tricks, and deceiving maneuvers." The synonyms for the word *wiles* in the thesaurus are "to scheme, connive, conspire, or devise." It can be a trick! It can be a maneuver! The devil is out to trick us into furthering his kingdom. He does this by getting us to think his thoughts and speak them out of our mouths. He puts together schemes so we will no longer further the Kingdom of God in our lives, but his kingdom.

The devil's words of suggestion come at us all day long. Included with the words *scheme* or *wiles* is the word *entice*. *Entice* means "to beguile, deceive, delude, trick, captivate, or distract." These *schemes* and *wiles* are an enticement to us to go another direction and turn away from God. It is within our free will to dominate our soul and allow the suggestions to go right by us. We do not ever have to give place to the devil's schemes, wiles, or enticements. The *armor of God* is described in Ephesians 6:10–18 (NKJV):

> *Finally, my brethren, be strong in the Lord and in the power of His might. Put on the whole armor of God, that ye may be able to stand against the wiles of the devil. For we do not wrestle against flesh and blood, but against principalities, against powers, against the rulers of the darkness of this age, against spiritual hosts of wickedness in the heavenly places. Therefore, take unto you the whole armor of God that you may be able to withstand in the evil day, and having done all, to stand. Stand therefore, having girded your waist with truth, having put on the breastplate of righteousness, and having shod your feet with the preparation of the gospel of peace; above all, taking the shield of faith, with which you will be able to quench all the fiery darts of the wicked one. And take the helmet of salvation, and the sword of the Spirit, which is the word of God; praying always with all prayer and supplication in the Spirit, and watchful to this end with all perseverance and supplication for all the saints . . ."*

The armor of God is there for our protection. We already have been given every piece. We just have to recognize we have each piece and learn to use them. We have to practice using the sword, which is the Word of God. This verse is saying that we are to have our life-giving resources around us at all times for our protection.

> *Wherefore, take unto you the whole armor of God*
> *that you may be able to withstand in the evil day*
> *and having done all to stand. Stand, therefore hav-*
> *ing your loins gird about with truth.*

The loins are the reproductive area of the human body. They embody the life-giving resources based on truth. As truth propels us into more truth, we see wider spheres of truth. It also increases and multiplies in the lives of those our lives touch. We have the God-given ability to reproduce His life in other people, a vessel for God to flow through (2 Timothy 2:21). He has given us His life, and if we are reproducing truth, we will see things correctly. The Holy Spirit, who is the *Spirit of Truth,* will give us understanding about what is happening in our lives.

When we have spent time with the Holy Spirit receiving revealed knowledge regarding His role in bringing us into truth, it is understood for all time. We are not left alone to find truth for ourselves. He is the *Spirit of Truth,* and it is His ministry to guide us into all truth. We will bear witness to the truth in our spirit.

And having on the breastplate of righteousness...

Righteousness is our right standing with God. It is His favor toward us. The fact is we have all the grace of God toward us and all the blessings toward us that we will ever need. Every divine provision has already been given to us. God's answers to us are *yes* and *amen.* We have all the promises of His Kingdom within us. When the Word says we are to seek first the Kingdom of God and His righteousness (Matthew 6:33), this means we are to seek Jesus' righteousness and His provisions within our spirit-man. His righteousness is His rightness, and His ministry is to show us how to be right. The Holy Spirit receives Jesus' character, and He will show it to us. In John 16:14 Jesus talks about the Holy Spirit:

He shall glorify me: for he shall receive of mine, and
shall shew it unto you.

The Holy Spirit wants to show us how to have the right mentality toward God and toward those around us. When Jesus came and died for us, we received His abundant life. The Holy Spirit wants to show us how Jesus would live out that abundant life through us. When we seek the Kingdom of God first within us and *mentally* wear the breastplate of His righteousness, it covers all the vital organs of our spirit-man and we are protected from the fiery darts of the evil one.

Your feet are shod with the preparation of the gospel
of peace.

The Bible says we are already seated in heavenly places in Christ Jesus. If we are, then all of this life on earth is already under our feet in the spiritual realm. We have already arrived in the spirit and need to realize this no matter what the circumstances look like around us. Our feet are protected or shod, and everywhere our feet go, we bring to that place the gospel of peace. We are messengers of peace and ambassadors of peace, bringing the peace of God to every place. This is why the devil attacks our soul so fiercely. He does not want us to know that we have defenses against his wiles. He wants us to feel vulnerable, fearful, and beaten down.

Above all, taking the shield of faith, wherewith
ye shall be able to quench all the fiery darts of the
wicked.

The shield of faith is out in front of us, and it covers us from the top of our head to the bottom of our feet. The men of war in ancient times had leather shields, and they soaked them in water before going into battle. When the shield was wet, it quenched the fiery darts that pierced it. If we have a shield of faith out in front of us, it will stop every fiery dart that comes at us. This is why it is important to know that we have the shield of faith. God has equipped us with the shield of faith. He has not left us in an exposed state; he has not left us without protection.

How does this work? It says in James 4:7, *"Submit to the Lord, resist the devil and he will flee from you."* If we always hold out in front of us a consciousness of who we are in Christ like a shield, then when the devil comes to us, it will be easy to resist him. But it is only by first submitting to the Lord and by taking Him at His Word that the devil can be resisted. Notice the order in the verse. First comes the submitting and then the resisting. We cannot resist him in our own strength.

Submitting is also one of the highest forms of praise. The Bible says that He inhabits the praises of His people (Psalm 22:3). When we praise God, we call Him on the scene and the devil is automatically resisted. The devil has to flee! In fact, the devil hates hearing praises to God so much that if we want to get rid of the devil quickly, start praising God. The devil cannot stand to be near anyone praising God. He will flee from us!

In verse 16 of Ephesians 6, the phrase *above all* has been important instruction to me. When I recognize I am not operating in faith but in fear, I stop what I am doing and find Scriptures that I can apply to my immediate situation. The Scriptures bring peace to my mind because the words are full of faith. Faith-filled words found in Scripture counteract distressing fear-filled thoughts. And whenever I do this, the Holy Spirit also shows me where my thinking needs to be to regain my total peace of mind. I purposely counter the pictures of failure the devil brings to me with pictures of success from the Scriptures. Even if I know deep down that my mind is not yet totally settled in a particular situation, I declare I have received revelation knowledge from the Holy Spirit, in Jesus' Name. My job is to recognize where I am, and His ministry is to move me to a place of total peace of mind where I can be completely settled in my soul and thereby gain the victory.

And take the helmet of salvation, and the sword of the Spirit, which is the word of God.

The helmet is a form of protection for our thinking processes. If we know without a doubt the price Jesus paid for us, it will be a protection for us. He was our substitute, and He gave us salvation. Remember that the Greek word for salvation is *sozo* and it means *"healed, delivered, made whole, restored and preserved."* The helmet of salvation means we are healed in body and mind, delivered from bondage, made whole or complete in Him, and preserved for future use. We are not unarmed. We have the Word of God, which is the sword of the spirit, but we have to use it effectively, not just batting it in the air.

When we pray, our words must have substance and be based on Scripture. Pray the Word to be really effective in spiritual warfare. This gives God the legal entry into our lives and situations. Our words give Him the authority to come on the scene and fight for us. Using Scripture arms Him for the battle. Remember, the battle is His but the victory is ours! Our weapons and ammunition are the Word. As much as He has compassion for what we are going through, if we do not give Him the legal right to come into our lives, He cannot do it. By using His words, we give Him the legal right and legal grounds to fight for us.

> *Praying always with all prayer and supplication in the spirit and watching thereunto with all perseverance and supplication for all saints.*

This is called intercession. We need to be persistent and humbly speak forth the will of God for our fellow brothers and sisters in the body of Christ. Whenever we see a need in someone's life, go to prayer and intercede for them.

According to 2 Corinthians 10:4–6, we are to pull down strongholds. A stronghold is like a fort, a fortress, or a citadel. In the dictionary, it says a *stronghold* is "a place where a group of people having certain views and attitudes are concentrated." When we do not cast down these imaginations, they gradually group themselves together and become high things that exalt themselves against the knowledge of God. All of a sudden, we have a platform in our thinking on which these thoughts and images have attached themselves. With each new image, the platform gets higher as they adhere to the previous one and build on the platform in our thinking.

Recognize that the first mind trap we take creates a foundation or platform in our mind and in our reasoning. This foundation will eventually grow and have walls that form chambers. It will even have a door with a lock in it, like an ancient citadel. This fortress will be located in one area of our mind, but since mind traps are constantly being suggested to us by the devil, he will have us building fortresses in many areas of our mind. He will give us many opportunities to build onto these foundations until they form a stronghold. A stronghold is a place of resistance. It is where we have concentrated our views, our philosophies, and reasoning. The Word tells us we are to pull down these places that resist God's plans of transformation for us.

Second Corinthians 10:3–6 shows us how to pull down these places of resistance and gives scriptural principles for our defense against wrong imaginations that can become idols:

> *For though we walk in the flesh, we do not war after the flesh: For the weapons of our warfare are not carnal, but mighty through God to the pulling down of strong holds; Casting down imaginations, and every high thing that exalteth itself against the knowledge of God, and bringing into captivity every thought to the obedience of Christ; and having in a readiness to revenge all disobedience, when your obedience is fulfilled.*

We cannot fight in our own strength. We cannot fight with our carnal thinking. Our warfare must be directed against the spiritual forces that are operating against us. We must cast down the imaginations and the high things that are trying to usurp our God-consciousness. When we recognize that our thinking is not in obedience to Christ and His Word, we must take authority over it by casting it out of our mind. We cast it out by speaking directly to the high thing or imagination and saying, "Spirit of fear or spirit of resentment, you have no part of me." Call it by name, whatever it is that is harassing you in your thinking and say, "You are cast out of my mind! My soul belongs to Jesus, and I have His peace reigning in my life, in Jesus' Name."

1.   How do we keep from idols?

_____

2.   Why is the armor of God important to our victory?

_____

3.   What is the cost of idolatry?

_____

4.   In Galatians, who are the partners of idolatry?

_____

5.   How do we combat idols?

_____

For though we walk in the flesh, we do not war
after the flesh. For the weapons of our warfare are
not carnal, but mighty through God to the pulling
down of strongholds: Casting down imaginations,
and every high thing that exalteth itself against the
knowledge of God, and bringing into captivity every
thought to the obedience of Christ. And having in
a readiness to revenge all disobedience, when your
obedience is fulfilled.
                              —2 Corinthians 10:3–6 (KJV)

Roll your works upon the Lord – commit and trust
them wholly to Him; [He will cause your thoughts
to become agreeable to His will, and] so shall your
plans be established and succeed.
                              —Proverbs 16:3 (AMPC)

God's Word calls us to be a light to the world around us, bright
beams of hope in a world consumed by fear. We are also to be the salt

of the earth, salt being a preservative to be applied to the corruption and pollution all around us. We are to throw a life preserver to those who are *going under* because of the mind games and mind traps people play and fall into.

Words create thoughts, and thoughts create images. Every word we hear creates an image in our minds. Every time we hear words, we imagine something and have a whole thought process that goes along with that image.

We have many Scriptures in the Word revealing God's thoughts toward us. God knows the thoughts of men, and there are Scriptures indicating the thoughts of both the wicked and the righteous man. In Genesis 50:20 (NIV), we read Joseph's words describing what his brothers did to him: *"You intended to harm me, but God intended it for good to accomplish what is now being done, the saving of many lives."* Joseph's brothers came against him and sold him into slavery. They did this because they were jealous and angry with him for being their father's favorite son and for the dreams he shared with them. When they conceived evil thoughts about him, there was an evil image made against him in their minds. But God used the evil his brothers did against him and turned it for good to save Israel during the years of famine.

In Joseph's case, persecution stole his home life from him. When his brothers sold him into slavery as a teenager, he was taken to Egypt. He did not see his father or his home for many years. This was the work of the devil, but Joseph kept a good attitude throughout his entire persecution. And God was with him and gave him favor in the eyes of those his life touched along the way. Joseph's brothers hurt him and betrayed him, but Joseph did not harbor bitter resentment against them. He is an example to us of how to maintain ourselves during a time of persecution and what to do when the temptation to feel sorry for ourselves comes.

Since he was betrayed and rejected, he is like a hope-setter for us. We have to realize that if he could make it through his persecutions, then we can make it through ours too. If God got him out of his persecution and made his situation better, then He can do the same for us. God turned the situation around for Joseph so that his latter end was better than his former.

In contrast to Joseph's case, Job's problem was that he did not have his enemy identified. While Joseph clearly identified his enemy as evil intent and not his brothers, Job was thinking and believing that God gives and God takes away. He blamed God for his losses. As long as he kept thinking it was God's doing, he was identifying God as his adversary. Until he changed his thinking and his words, he was trapped in his circumstances by his reasoning. Many people still believe that God is the source of the losses and destruction in their lives. They still think like Job. They need to identify their enemy as the devil and not God.

In Job 21:27 we read, *"Behold I know your thoughts and the devices which you wrongfully imagine against me."* Job started to realize and say regarding his so-called friends: *"All the things you are saying are not upholding me, they are not helping me. They are wrong images of me."* Then he identified God in his life when he went on to say, *"But this is where God is."*

Job 42:2–6 says in the Living Bible:

> *I know that you can do anything, and that no one can stop you. You ask who it is who has so foolishly denied your providence. It is I. I was talking about things I knew nothing about and did not under-stand things far too wonderful for me. [You said,] "Listen and I will speak! Let me put the questions to you! See if you can answer them!" [But now I say,] "I had heard about you before, but now I have seen you, and I loathe myself and repent in dust and ashes."*

As soon as Job started to see who God was and where He was in the situation, he started to pull out of his misery. That was when the blessings of God could overtake him and bless him. While he was debating and rationalizing everything that his friends said to him, he held himself in a position of confusion.

Going over and over a situation in our minds only results in mental striving, and we become stuck. There has to come a point in time when we start to live by faith. God will let us stay in the pit we have dug for ourselves as long as we want to stay there. When we have had enough, we can come out. But to come out, we have to say, "These are not God's thoughts toward me." We need to ask ourselves, "What would Jesus do in this situation?" When the light comes into our situation, it is at that point we start to climb out of our pit (Psalm 119:130).

The Holy Spirit will always be there to help us and to teach us how to get out of the pit, but we have to decide to change our thinking. The Holy Spirit is a gentleman, and He will never force His thinking on our minds. He will wait until we have had enough and are ready to turn to Him.

First Chronicles 28:9 says:

> *And thou, Solomon my son, know thou the God of thy father, and serve him with a perfect heart and with a willing mind: for the Lord searcheth all hearts, and understandeth all the imaginations of the thoughts: if thou seek him, he will be found of thee; but if thou forsake him, he will cast thee off forever.*

In this passage, David tells his son Solomon about God's character. God does not knock on people's doors and say, "Hello, I'm God. Serve Me!" He allows people to go by their own choices and devices. He never forces His way on anyone. God knows all our thoughts and the images those thoughts are creating, and God understands all the thoughts and imaginations of our hearts.

First Chronicles 29:18 says, *"O Lord God of Abraham, Isaac, and of Israel, our fathers, keep this forever in the imagination of the thoughts of the heart of the people, and prepare their heart unto thee."*

Here, in David's prayer, is another example of imaginations coming as a result of the thoughts of the heart. Words create thoughts, thoughts create images, and images form philosophies, which in turn build strongholds. This is the natural progression of how our mind operates.

God is omniscient or all-knowing, and He knows the thoughts of men. Man cannot hide any thought from God. Man cannot have any private or secret thoughts that God does not recognize. Jesus also said many times in the New Testament that He knew men's thoughts, and He knew the evil they planned in their hearts.

Matthew 12:25 says, *"And Jesus knew their thoughts, and said unto them, Every kingdom divided against itself is brought to desolation, and every city or house divided against itself shall not stand . . ."*

Our body is our house (earth-suit). Our spirit and soul reside within our body. In order for our house to stand, our spirit and our soul must be united. They must be working together. They cannot be divided against each other if we want to occupy our own house in peace.

"Every kingdom divided against itself is brought to desolation." When the spirit and the soul are divided, we are headed toward death and desolation. *"And every city or house divided against itself shall not stand."* God says the same thing in James 1:8, "A double-minded man is unstable in all his ways." No wonder! When a person is double minded, their goal will surely die because their life force is cut off at their neck. The thinking in their soul is in direct conflict with God's Word in their heart, so they are torn and conflicted. They will waiver, hesitate, and not know what to do. The Word is called the anchor to the soul (Hebrews 6:19). The Word holds our soul from drifting away from God. But if the spirit and the soul are divided, the anchor cannot hold our soul in submission to our spirit. Our soul will ascend above our spirit and rule over it with wrong thoughts. Nor should our soul be generating of itself. It must come under the control of our spirit.

Proverbs 4:20–22 states:

> *My son, attend to my words, incline thine ear unto my sayings. Let them not depart from thine eyes; keep them in the midst of thine heart. For they are life unto those that find them, and health to all their*

*flesh. Keep thy heart with all diligence; for out of it
are the issues of life.*

From our heart or spirit will flow the issues of life. It will hold
us, but we have to do our part to maintain our peace. We have to
keep ourselves when thoughts come by saying, "These thoughts have
condemnation on them. These are not my thoughts!" Or we might
realize our thoughts have *obligation* on them. God does not want
us to do things for people out of blind obligations to our impulsive
promises or their selfish demands. We can discern and reject these
negative and destructive thoughts. If we do, the life force within us
can flow freely from our spirit and hold our soul in peace in any
situation.

Proverbs 16:3 in the *Amplified Bible* says:

*Roll your works upon the Lord—commit and trust
them wholly to Him; [He will cause your thoughts
to become agreeable to His will, and] so shall your
plans be established and succeed.*

This is where we want our thoughts to be. We want them to be
established in God. This is the picture of trust and submission that
God desires for us. The reward is that our thoughts will be in line
with God's will for our life. It takes discipline to hold our minds in
line with the Word of God. The key is in the knowing that God has
made a path of success for us in every situation.

1. Why is it important to bring our thoughts under control?

    _____

2. Does God cause the circumstances to teach us?

    _____

3. When will God bring us out of a situation?

    _____

4. What is the Holy Spirit's ministry in overcoming a circumstance?

    _____

5. How can we avoid being double-minded?

    _____

CHAPTER 6

Mind Traps vs. the Love of God

1 Corinthians 13:4–8 (AMPC); Philippians 1:6

All the mind traps that I have isolated operate against the love of God. First Corinthians 13:4–8 in the *Amplified Bible* reads:

> *Love endures long and is patient and kind; love never is envious nor boils over with jealousy; is not boastful or vain glorious, does not display itself haughtily. It is not conceited—arrogant, and inflated with pride; it is not rude (unmannerly), and does not act unbecomingly. Love [God's love in us] does not insist on its own rights or its own way, for it is not self-seeking; it is not touchy or fretful or resentful; it takes no account of the evil done to it— pays no attention to a suffered wrong. It does not rejoice at injustice and unrighteousness, but rejoices when right and truth prevail. Love bears up under anything and everything that comes, is ever ready to believe the best of every person, its hopes are fadeless under all circumstances and it endures everything*

[without weakening]. Love never fails—never fades
out or becomes obsolete or comes to an end.

God desires us to think with love, speak with love, listen with love, and to act with love. Then we can know our faith will work since faith works by love. If we are not getting answers to our prayers, we must not only look at how much faith we are exercising, but we have to look at how much love we have in our hearts and lives. We have to look at our attitudes.

If I have asked for something in Jesus' Name and I am waiting for it for years and at the same time I have turmoil and discord within and around me, it could be a clue that the spirit realm is being hindered. Many times, it is not even the devil who has hindered our answers to prayer, but we become the main hindrance to our prayers being answered. Sometimes we are so deceived by our own attitudes of self-defense and self-righteousness that God cannot work in our lives.

On the other hand, I can stand for years believing for something from God and have perfect peace in my mind. This is a sure sign that I am in His will—when I have His peace. There is no need to be impatient because I know the answer to my prayer has an appointed time in the natural realm. When the devil applies pressure against my faith and challenges what I have believed and received (taken) from the spirit realm, I can easily answer with the Word. Each time I respond to the devil with the Word, I gain strength in spiritual combat. Eventually, it is going to become easy to avoid his mind traps.

When Jesus was tempted by the devil in the wilderness for forty days and forty nights, He answered each time by quoting Scripture to him. Jesus used the sword of the Spirit, which is the Word of God, and we need to do the same thing. I stood for years for certain things and knew that they were mine. During the wait, I was victorious within my spirit and in my everyday life.

The mind traps of *expectation* and *assumption* are contrary to the love of God because they are self-seeking and self-centered. These two insist on their own rights. They are looking to man or circumstances for approval and acceptance. When a person becomes developed in the self-centeredness of these two mind traps, they enter into codependency. A codependent person looks to others outside of themselves for their emotional well-being.

Recall, projecting, and the *cares of this world* are also contrary to the love of God. *Recall* will remember every evil that was ever done to it. *Recall* pays attention to a suffered wrong and will project a negative expectation into the future and see it come to pass as it did in the past. With negative *recall,* we remember the acts done to us, and with *projecting* we anticipate the evil that is going to come to us in the future. When we are in these mind traps, it is impossible to believe the best in every person or in every situation, as the love of God requires. When *cares of this world* consume our thinking, we have focused our attention on the problems in the natural realm. In this mind trap, we have lost all hope. There is no way of believing the best in every person or situation.

Comparison and *pride* also work against the love of God. The love of God is not boastful or vainglorious. It is not haughty, arrogant, conceited, or inflated with pride. The person who has allowed the *comparison* mind trap to overtake them will come underneath whomever or whatever they are comparing themselves to and feel less than or inferior to them. This is not where God wants us to be as His child. When well established in the mind trap of *comparison,* the pressure to keep up with the Joneses will lead to compulsive spending or other compulsive lifestyles. Each material item that is acquired will be coveted and spoken of in a boastful manner. The hidden motive is always acceptance and approval from man based on the amount and kind of material possessions accumulated. This person becomes boastful and vainglorious, is inflated with pride, and will display themselves haughtily, arrogantly, and with conceit.

With the mind traps of *impulsiveness* and *deceitfulness of riches,* we will also find conceit and arrogance, along with rudeness and acting unbecomingly. People who are caught up in *deceitfulness of riches* have grandiose mentalities. They suffer from delusions of grandeur. They think they are better than anyone else, and they put all their trust in riches. Those inflated with pride and those who walk in impulsiveness can be very rude, demanding, and unmannerly. People trapped in both *impulsiveness* and *deceitfulness of riches* act unbecomingly since they want their own way at everyone else's expense.

When a person falls into the mind traps of *affliction* and *persecution*, they endure for a time and then become offended. People who are in *persecution* are very touchy, fretful, or resentful. When they are being persecuted for the Word or for their beliefs, they become easily offended. They cannot endure long. They go into resentment and develop bitterness toward God or they fall into self-pity. When they have afflictions and pressures and God is not answering them the way they think He should be answering them, they become impatient and unkind. But the love of God is not envious; the love of God is not unkind; and it is not touchy, fretful, or resentful.

The *lusts of other things* or desires of other things also insist on their own rights and their own way. In this trap, a person wants other things instead of desiring God. They are seeking their own way.

People who are caught up in the mind traps of *intellectualizing* and *spiritualizing* rejoice at injustice or unrighteousness. They will try to rectify the situation by rationalizing an act of injustice to make it seem right in their own minds, or they will water down an act of injustice or unrighteousness by having an alibi or excuse for it in their own thinking. They secretly rejoice because they have turned a situation around for their own selfish purposes. They will try to keep doing things their own way. Yet they will never reach the place of truth in a situation while they continue to *intellectualize* or *spiritualize* because they are so deep in self-deception.

All these mind traps keep us from walking in the love of God, and they keep us from being in the rest of God. Each trap becomes an idol in the mind because it puts *self* on the throne and keeps us in offense, rejection, and depression. These are extremely self-defeating idols that hold many people in bondage, but we can be delivered from them and learn to avoid giving them place in our lives. Joshua 24:15 says, "Choose us this day who we will serve." God created man as a free moral agent. As a free moral agent, God will never force His will on us! He will never go over our will. He waits for us to get to the place where we realize that we need Him. The dilemma for mankind is we cannot get to this place by ourselves. We need His Word and the revelation of the Holy Spirit. With His Word light enters, it dispels the darkness and delivers us. The Holy Spirit also brings the light to show us areas for deliverance by bringing us the knowledge and understanding of our situations. He wants us to be free. Philippians 1:6 has always been a comforting verse to me: *"Being confident of this very thing, that he which hath begun a good work in you will perform it until the day of Jesus Christ."*

We are to walk in the confidence that the work the Holy Spirit has already begun in us; He will perform it. The experience of regeneration or being *born again* makes the Word of God come alive to us. The Bible becomes a different book after salvation has occurred. Our job is to cooperate with the Holy Spirit and not hinder Him. A speaker I once heard said, "God is not looking for gold or silver vessels, but yielded ones." This thought has stayed with me and has guided my attitude toward God's work in my life. We can be very spiritually dense at times, but God understands this. We must also understand and accept that we are on a learning curve. We have to be patient with ourselves. God does not give up on us, and we should not give up on ourselves either. But here it all depends on our own choice whether we experience life or death in our daily walk.

1. When does the love walk begin in us?

   _____

2. How do we increase in the love of God?

   _____

3. How did Jesus defeat the devil in the wilderness?

   _____

4. How do we choose who we will serve?

   _____

SECTION II

DISCOVERING THE
MIND TRAPS

INTRODUCTION

Each mind trap in this book is shared in the order I experienced them. The first five traps were revealed to me in quick succession because God did not want me to hinder His work in my life. God was working to recover our marriage. Becoming aware of these wiles suggested by the devil has kept me in control of my own thoughts, and knowing them even today allows me not to give him any place. It has been a life-changing experience for me. The Holy Spirit has been faithful to teach me how to get out of each one of the mind traps. It is not that mind traps never come to me anymore, but now I am able to identify them much faster. I can still get tripped up if I choose to dethrone Jesus in my thinking. The goal is to allow myself not to continue in wrong thinking until I am all the way into depression but to catch myself earlier at the place of rejection or offense, or better yet, to even hear and see ahead of time where the wrong thinking will lead me and then choose not to allow it to entrap my mind. When I learned to recognize the wrong-thinking patterns, I was able to stop the step-by-step progression of the mind trap into offense, into rejection, and eventually into depression.

Each mind trap in this book is given with a biblical example showing the mind trap, the offense, and rejection that are involved. Sometimes we can even hear depression speaking in the person's words. I have also included some of my own experiences and those of the women I have known over the years from my Bible study group. It is my prayer that this material will open our hearts and minds to new ways of thinking and will show us how to recognize our own wrong-thinking patterns that habitually lead us into depression. Since Jesus has already bought and paid the price on the cross for the rest in our souls, may He also, through this material, expose the idols in our lives that are hindering us from entering and staying in His rest.

CHAPTER 1

Expectation

Proverbs 23:17–18; John 16:33

The synonyms in the *Corel Word Perfect 8 Thesaurus* for *expectation* are "to anticipate, foresee, imagine and wait." The *Webster's New World Dictionary* defines *expectation* as "a looking for as due, proper, or necessary; a thing looking forward to. To look for as likely to appear or occur." (All future references to the thesaurus and the dictionary in later chapters will be quoted from these two sources.)

Expectations are placed on people, on circumstances, and even on ourselves. As we have all experienced, people and circumstances are not reliable sources for our expectations. God is the only absolute, and He is our only reliable source. He gives us His blueprint for our lives in His Word. One acronym for the word *Bible* is Basic Instructions before Leaving Earth. When we take Him at His Word, we are dealing with His goals for our lives and they are for us to experience success.

Proverbs 23:17–18 shows where our expectations must be: "*Let not thine heart envy sinners: but be thou in the fear of the Lord all the day long. For surely there is an end; and thine expectation shall not be cut off.*"

It is easy to look at people and envy their possessions or their successes. However, it is only a trap to take our attention away from reverencing God who wants to give us all things that pertain to life and godliness (2 Peter 1:3). God says our expectations will not be cut off as long as they are in Him and His Word. God wants us to put our expectations in Him because He is faithful and dependable. He will never let us down.

There is a right thinking and a wrong thinking regarding expectation. One scriptural example showing right thinking on expectation is found in Philippians 3:20, "But our citizenship is in heaven and we eagerly await the Savior from there, the Lord Jesus Christ." Another is in Titus 2:13: "Looking for that blessed hope, and the glorious appearing of the great God and our Savior Jesus Christ." God wants us to *expect* that Jesus is coming back. This is a good expectation. When life gives us opportunities for defeat, we are to have our minds on Ephesians 2:6, which says, "We are already seated in heavenly places in Christ Jesus." If we are already in a seated position, this means we have also *ceased* from laboring over difficulties in this life. He is now seated at the right hand of the Father. Difficulties may still be going on, but we must realize they are only *temporary*. They are subject to change by the Word of God.

> *While we look not at the things which are seen, but at the things which are not seen: for the things which are seen are temporal; but the things which are not seen are eternal.* (2 Cor. 4:18)

> *Now thanks be unto God, which always causeth us to triumph in Christ, and maketh manifest the savour of his knowledge by us in every place.* (2 Cor. 2:14)

God always causes us to triumph in every situation. When we come on the scene, God comes with us and His knowledge or presence and influence is felt in every place. We cannot expect our lives to be a bed of roses. And never think, *I'm going to walk through this trial,*

and afterward everything will be fine, and I'm going to go to heaven.
No. It is our job to enforce what Jesus has already accomplished in
this life. God wants us to live as conquerors and victors. We are to
appropriate the Word of God and take authority over everything
that comes our way. It is imperative that we build the Word of God
into our spirits daily so we are prepared when difficulties knock on
our door. The Father does guarantee all the works of the enemy are
defeated and He is with us on the way out of every test, temptation,
or trial. We can look at these as difficulties or opportunities since we
are on enemy turf, but with our minds fixed on the things we have
been given from above, we can overcome this world system of thinking and watch the Word work for us.

Jesus said He has already overcome the world in John 16:33:
*"These things I have spoken unto you, that in me ye might have peace. In
the world ye shall have tribulation: but be of good cheer; I have overcome
the world."*

By placing our hopes and expectations in the unsure hands of
people, we can expect them to be stepped on, ignored, misplaced or
even taken from us. Jesus' words should prepare us to live in the real
world. He said to expect tribulation but to remember that He has
already overcome everything in our lives that we will ever experience.

Circumstances are just as variable as people because people are
involved in circumstances. Why do we have to experience this over
and over again before we finally get the message? Why do we continue to make the same mistakes? The answer lies in our motives.
The Bible talks about the hidden motives of the heart, and sometimes they are so well hidden that even we do not know what they
are. The most common motive behind misplaced expectation is a
codependent desire for acceptance and approval from others. As long
as we need the approval and acceptance of others, we will place our
expectation on them, instead of on God.

The Biblical example of this is seen in Matthew 26:31–35. Jesus
is speaking to the disciples about his eventual death. He says, *"For
it is written: I will strike the shepherd and the sheep of the flock will be
scattered."* Peter is appalled at this thought and answers, *"Even if all
fall away on account of you, I never will."* This seems very noble; how-

ever, let's analyze it by our premise on expectation. His expectation is that he will not fall away, even if the others do. Does he trust in God to bring this to pass or in himself? When we have self-expectation, there is usually self-perfection, self-performance, and self-pressure to perform and stay perfect. God's Word said, *"All would fall away,"* but Peter is contradicting Jesus and saying the opposite. Obviously, his expectation is not placed on God; therefore, it must be on himself.

How about his motives? They seem good, but if his motives were to protect Jesus' interests, wouldn't he have said something like, "I'll stop them from being offended, Lord," or "Don't worry, I'll gather them back again." Instead, he said, *"They might be offended, but I certainly won't!"* This shows Peter's desire for approval from Jesus by exalting himself above the others. Unfortunately, Peter's self-expectation was not fulfilled, and he did become offended and denied the Lord three times as foretold. We can also see rejection and depression took hold of his thinking as he separated himself from the other disciples.

A key example of an expectation on people is in the account of Naaman in 2 Kings. He was the army captain of the king of Syria. He almost missed his healing because of his expectations. Naaman knew through his wife's maid that there was a prophet in Israel who could heal him of his leprosy. He sent a messenger to the king of Israel, but the king assumed Naaman was looking to him to act as God and heal him of his leprosy. Elisha the prophet stepped in after hearing the king of Israel moaning. Verses 9-14 give the account of Naaman's expectation, offense, and rejection statements.

> *So Naaman came with his horses and with his chariot, and stood at the door of the house of Elisha. And Elisha sent a messenger unto him, saying Go and wash in Jordan seven times, and thy flesh shall come again to thee, and thou shalt be clean. But Naaman was wroth, and went away, and said, Behold, I thought, He will surely come out to me, and stand, and call on the name of the Lord his God, and strike his hand over the place, and recover the leper. Are*

not Abana and Pharpar, rivers of Damascus, better than all the waters of Israel? May I not wash in them, and be clean? So he turned and went away in a rage. And his servants came near, and spake unto him, and said, My father, if the prophet had bid thee do some great thing, wouldest thou not have done it? How much rather then, when he saith to thee, wash, and be clean? Then went he down, and dipped himself seven times in Jordan, according to the saying of the man of God: and his flesh came again like unto the flesh of a little child, and he was clean. (2 Kings 5:9–14)

Naaman was cleansed of his leprosy by simply obeying Elisha's instructions. Yet he almost missed his healing because of his expectations. Naaman expected Elisha to deal with him directly. When Elisha sent a messenger instead, Naaman was offended. He felt rejected by the instructions he was given because he compared the little rivers of Israel with the big rivers of his country. They seemed of no consequence in his eyes.

Verse 11 gives the account of Naaman's preconceived image or expectation. This is what he thought would happen when he was healed. He thought the prophet would come out to him and call on the name of the Lord, wave his hand over the place, and heal him of his leprosy. When his expectation was not met, he was offended and took on defeat and failure. Finally, his servants talked him into doing exactly what the prophet said to do. They saved him from his preconceived expectations. He was healed of his leprosy by his obedience to Elisha's instructions to dip himself in the Jordan River seven times.

Expectation on other people can be just as grievous as self-expectation and expectation on circumstances. Ephesians 2:10 tells us that we are God's workmanship or masterpiece. We must realize we are approved of God and accepted by Him. This truth should determine our well-being. In my marriage, I made the mistake of giving my husband the job of determining my well-being. I expected him to praise me for my efforts in our home. I built my identity on what he said about me. Consequently, whenever my cheerleader did not feel like waving his pom-poms and giving me the much needed recognition I craved, I was crushed. One evening, the Holy Spirit exposed this error in my thinking and delivered me from the expectation mind trap.

One night, Dennis and I were watching a movie on TV. As I became involved with the actors and the plot, the message infiltrated my thinking. I found myself comparing my husband to the leading man on the screen, and I thought, *Why doesn't Dennis love me like that?* Later on, I thought, *Dennis should love me like that!* By the time the movie was over, I thought, *Dennis is going to love me like that!* I formed an expectation of my husband from the leading man's actions.

After the movie, I labored with my bedtime preparations. I fluffed my hair and chose my most alluring negligee. All this time I went over in my mind how the leading man looked and what he said. When my careful ritual was finally completed, I made my grand entrance into the bedroom. Apparently, I had taken too long because the sound of surprised pleasure I had expected to come out of my husband's mouth sounded more like a yawn. All he said was, "What's this all about?"

Looking back, I realized I would have settled for any expression of love but it was not to be. To say my feelings were hurt is an understatement! I felt crushed, rejected, and on my way to depression. But this time, I asked God to show me how I got into this *all-too familiar* place. By His Spirit, I was given a replay of the entire evening and I saw where I made my mistake. My expectation for our relationship was not placed on God but on Dennis. Love needs time to grow, and I was not patient enough to give God time to work in Dennis's heart. This was only months after we resumed our marriage following a time of separation. My hidden motive was to feel approved and accepted by him, but the expectation mind trap got me because I wanted him to perform like the actor on the screen.

God showed me that I was His workmanship in His Beloved (Ephesians 2:10) and that I was blessed by Him, approved and accepted by Him (Ephesians 1:6). I had to remind myself that if

God tells me that I am accepted by Him, then I am, whether I feel like I am or not. I saw that God loved me and I was His glory in Christ Jesus. Even if Dennis never realized this, it did not alter who I really was in God's eyes. I needed to draw my identity from God, not from Dennis. This was a life-changing revelation for me, one that helped me get my expectation off Dennis and onto God. I realized my acceptance and approval by God was secure in Christ. Our pastor also shared with us there were three F's we needed to apply to our lives. They are *facts* of the Word of God, *faith* in the facts of the Word of God, and then come *feelings*. I had been living up to this time in my life by feelings, which are based on emotions and are variable. By taking only the facts and putting my faith in the facts, I was on a much more solid foundation. I still live my life fasting feelings, which means feelings are not my primary source for truth.

As we saw earlier, the mind traps are all contrary to the love of God since they all exalt the selfish nature. Expectation thinking says, "I am self-centered. Therefore, I will be self-seeking. I will seek my own rights. I will allow my thoughts to expect approval and wait for acceptance from a certain person, or the way I *image* or imagine a circumstance to turn out." Because we are expecting our own preconceived outcome, we will receive acceptance or approval only when the circumstance turns out the way we imagined it would. This is the way the expectation mind trap works, and it is the thinking needed to form codependency. In a codependent relationship, there is the giver and the taker. The one who always gives may not feel they are being selfish but they really are since they would rather stay in the abusive relationship than leave or change. They are too selfish to give up the person. They want to keep the other person emotionally dependent on them.

This is also true of a parent who will not train or discipline their child because they do not want to incur their disapproval. If the parent does not stand up to the child, the child becomes the authority figure and the roles are reversed. It is a grave injustice to a child to not train them because the adult is codependent and needs the child's approval for their own worth. In this reversal of roles, we end up serving the devil, when all the while we think we are serving ourselves. When we do not set boundaries, we let the child become the parent and this causes them to be insecure.

Another hurtful side with parents and children is an expectation to perfection. Although the parents may have good intentions in their hearts, their approach and delivery is harmful to their children's spirits. God warned against this in Ephesians 6:4 and Colossians 3:21:

> *"And, ye fathers [parents] provoke not your children to wrath: but bring them up in the nurture and admonition of the Lord."*

> *"Fathers [parents] provoke not your children to anger, lest they be discouraged."*

The Amplified version says it best:

> *"Fathers, do not provoke or irritate or fret your children [do not be hard on them or harass them], lest they become discouraged and sullen and morose and feel inferior and frustrated. [Do not break their spirit.]"*

Children desire security from their parents. Rightful correction in the nurture and admonition of the Lord will teach them to bend their wills toward God's will over time. We need to correct not punish since this is usually out of revenge and anger. The child's thinking will also need to be conformed, which rightful discipline and instruction will accomplish.

Fathers are to avoid severity, anger, harshness, and cruelty. When fathers abdicate their responsibility of child training to the mother, they usually end up with rebellious children.

Fathers must always stay in authority in the home and can delegate their authority to the mothers, but they must stay informed.

Perfection shows itself by these attitudes: irritability, agitation, intolerance, competition, superiority, criticism, pride, vanity, ego, anger and frustration (offense). Competition between the parents in child rearing will always put the children in authority, and they are not equipped for this responsibility. If our children are making statements such as, "Why are you always angry? Can't I do anything right in your eyes?" or if they are just outright rebellious, take a look at how they might be rejected by our words toward their spirits.

The account of David and Absalom is an example of harshness toward a child and the horrible rebellious conduct of a son toward his father. The account is in 2 Samuel 11:1–18:18. Here are the highlights showing the destructive attitudes and sins:

- David's failure with Bathsheba
- Amnon's sin with Tamar, David sidestepped punishment for Amnon's sin under the law (favoritism)
- Absalom killing Amnon
- Absalom flees to Geshur takes on expectation, offense, rejection, and defeat toward David who takes on pride and harshness in his refusal to see Absalom
- Absalom allows rebellion through deception, seduction, betrayal, treachery, conniving, flattery, false justice, conspiracy, usurping, and anarchy
- David flees and Absalom goes to Jerusalem
- Absalom killed, two sons of David lost

The expectation mind trap does not always take on such earth-shaking proportions. It can sometimes be the little expectations that trip us up the most. When someone tells us they will be in a certain place at a certain time and they do not show up, it can set us up for the expectation mind trap. The first time this happens, we may think they ran into some difficulty. The second time, we get a little miffed but we forgive them. The third, fourth, and fifth times, our resentment builds; and before we know it, we are angry and never going to trust them again.

This can be a difficult situation because we need to be able to believe the person's intentions are true and that we can believe their word. Our problem comes when we expect circumstances to be exactly the way they said they would be and then we find we cannot rely on them. Their words just cannot be trusted, and without realizing it, we have formed a mental image and set ourselves up for a disappointment. This is the subtle way the expectation mind trap operates.

A friend of mine stopped cooking dinner for her husband when she realized his remark, "I'll be home at six o'clock," really meant he would grab a sandwich at the office and make it home by nine. Her decision to stop cooking was not for revenge but simply to save herself time and disappointment. When we are in this kind of situation, we need to continually forgive the other person; otherwise, unforgiveness and resentment, which are characteristics of bitterness, will begin to add up. We place our expectation in God by praying for the individual to become a person of their word.

Next, we must check our motives. Are we angry because the person's treatment makes us feel unimportant or rejected? Then our approval and acceptance is probably based on them or the situation. This can never give us happiness since happiness comes from within. If we can identify with our true person, a new creature in Christ, and then take on the attributes Jesus gave us, we can start on the road to wholeness in Christ. We can avoid being offended by the thoughtless behavior of others.

I learned another subtle example of expectation while helping a friend who was getting trapped in anger. She was angry every time she talked to her parents, and it took her a few days to get over it and acquire back her peace of mind. She was at the point of not wanting to speak to them at all. They were constantly saying they were going to give money to her brother and sister and kept asking her for advice, but they never really took her advice. When she looked at her thinking and its effect on her emotions, she realized she was angry because she expected her parents to be able to say no to the constant begging for handouts and she expected them to stop and act differently. When they did not heed her advice to stop giving her siblings money, she became angry and got offended. Once she realized that they were working with the knowledge and ability they had, she was delivered from the expectation and the offense she felt. When she realized they could not even hear, let alone do, what she was telling them, she saved herself from experiencing anger and aggravation at them. She was then able to forgive them and pray for God's wisdom and the knowledge of His will to come to them. We cannot expect people to walk in knowledge they do not possess, nor can we expect people to walk in the same actions we would walk in. This is called expectation based on our own code of conduct and expectations on others to know better. How many times have we heard, "Well, they should know better!" Apparently they don't or they would walk in the knowledge. We have to give people the time they need to see another way of operating that isn't established in mind traps.

Here is another very common occurrence of a circumstance with the mind trap of expectation in it. We cut our time short with the person we are with in order to make a previously planned appointment, only to find the person does not want to do what we had both planned beforehand. My friend's daughter went back to her fiancé's apartment instead of going out to lunch with her mother because she had previous plans with him to buy new car tires that afternoon. She expected him to remember and be ready when she got there, but he was engrossed on the Internet and did not want to break away. She got upset because she missed having lunch with her mother and her expectation was not met. She had formed an image of what they would be doing that afternoon, and he disappointed her.

This is how an image of an expectation can lead to offense, and it all happened within her thinking. She took the mind trap of expectation and was offended. It was her responsibility instead not to form an expectation or get angry when her expectation was not met. It was not that her fiancé disappointed her as much as she had all her eggs, or *images*, in one basket! This is the time to make our minds stay neutral and not form images of any expected end. The disappointment comes when we are thinking how the change of plans is affecting us. When we recognize the opportunity to sin by putting *self* on the throne, choose to forgive the person and receive another time for new tires.

I have trained my mind to stay neutral, saving myself from many situations that could have caused me emotional hurt. It takes practice, but I was desperate to not live in hurt anymore. How desperate are we? Are we ready to remove the emotional *land mines* from our thinking? We need to start by taking our thinking seriously and stop being our own worst enemy.

Jesus encountered this mind trap in Nazareth when the town's people expected Him to not change. He was still Jesus, the carpenter's son and couldn't possibly be performing miracles in His heavenly Father's name. They missed out on receiving, except for a few, because of their expectation and offense, which led to their unbelief (Mark 6:1–6).

The whole book of Jonah is a great example of an expectation to evil. God sent Jonah to Nineveh to warn the people to turn away from their sins. Jonah, the prophet of the Lord, fled to Joppa and found a ship going to Tarshish, the most remote of the Phoenician trading places. He wanted no mercy to be shown for their wickedness. After the word of the Lord came to Jonah a second time, he went to Nineveh. The great city believed in God, the king proclaimed a fast, and the city repented. This offended Jonah since he said, "*You are a gracious God and merciful, slow to anger and of great kindness, and [when sinners turn to you and meet Your conditions] you revoke the (sentence of) evil against them* (Jonah 4:2, AMPC). Why are you willing to forgive for evil? We can ask the same question today when we retain evil against people who have mistreated us or had a judgment against us. The Lord says to us, as He did to Jonah, remit their sins and forgive so we can be set free. It doesn't matter whether the other person ever forgives. We need to be free today and not give place to the devil in our lives.

And like Jonah, let's not go into self-pity, which is a description of rejection and wanting to die, which is depression. This pattern of thinking can be costly to our spiritual well-being. It is a much better place to be in God's thinking, speaking, and acting, which in the long run won't cost us.

1.   Why do most people get offended?

_____

2.   How do we get ourselves into depression?

   _____

3.   Where should we put our expectation?

   _____

4.   Are we being selfish to think people will meet our expectations?

   _____

5.   When we become offended with a person, what went wrong?

   _____

6.   What if we become offended with a place, for example, a church?

   _____

7.   When it comes to expectation, why do people continue to make the same mistakes?

   _____

CHAPTER 2

Luke 15:11–32; Psalm 19:13

The synonyms for *assume* in the thesaurus are "to theorize, speculate and conjecture." The dictionary defines assuming as "the act of taking responsibility upon oneself, taking over or taking for granted." It is the act of drawing conclusions from certain evidences or supposing something to be a fact.

In each of the mind traps, I have explained both positive thinking and negative thinking. Each time we notice how the mind trap thinks, speaks, and acts. Assumption and persecution are the only ones where there is no positive side. There are no positive examples of assumption in the Bible or in everyday life. Maybe this is why the old saying for the word *assume* is, "Ass of you and me is what you make when you assume." This makes up the letters used in the word *assume*. Who wants to be a donkey anyway?

Assumption is a mind trap that the enemy uses to lead us down the path of defeat since we take for granted or suppose something to be a fact, when it is not. This has obvious dangers. In assumption, we also see the process of *jumping to conclusions* operating. We are misled by our own thinking, and we are in for a surprise! Assumption is often based on past experiences rather than on the present facts.

All the years of living with an alcoholic husband made it difficult for me to trust his words. Even after years had passed and we were both walking with the Lord and growing in Him, I found myself assuming the worst about him— even when he said to me "I love you." I would assume his intent was as a sister in the Lord, or I thought he was telling me this just to pacify me. I had a hard time believing his words.

The devil brings the image, but if we take it, it becomes our own and we become self-deceived. Needless to say, as long as I assumed his present sayings were like those of the past, I was not going to come to the place of trust and participate in our marriage. Instead, I was in a place of distrust because of the mind trap of assumption.

As soon as the Holy Spirit showed me what I was doing in my thinking, I repented and made a decision not to allow assumption to be part of my thinking again. I began to accept what Dennis said to me as the truth, and I became much happier in my marriage.

Another example of assumption that I saw happened while I was working as a supervisor. At the nursing agency was an incident that involved another supervisor's assistant. She was doing her best to be accepted by my assistant, and one day she took all of my assistant's new patient paperwork. Her intention was good, but her act of kindness had a price tag on it. She wanted to help my assistant with her workload, but what she was really looking for was acceptance from my assistant. The problem was no one knew why she was doing this, so her extra work went unappreciated. She felt rejected when she was not appreciated for her extra efforts. When my assistant did not give her the assumed response, she became angry and vowed never to help her again. This created a division in the office between the two assistants, and the emotional environment was full of the needless pain of rejection.

This is a common occurrence in offices everywhere. The other supervisor's assistant assumed she would be praised and accepted if she did my assistant's work for her. I saw from this experience that we cannot allow the seed of assumption to be planted in our thinking. Nor can we let the image of acceptance and approval for ourselves be in our thinking by taking upon ourselves a responsibility that is not our own.

An example of assumption is found in chapter 15 of Luke in the story of the prodigal son. The younger son went into the world and squandered his inheritance, yet his father's heart yearned for his return. The older son stayed home and played the role of the faithful son. He did everything that was expected of him around the household. When the prodigal returned in humility, his father greeted him with joy and forgiveness. But when the older brother heard the news, he became very upset. In Luke 15:29, he said to his father, *"Lo these many years do I serve thee, neither transgressed I at any time thy commandment; and yet thou never gavest me a kid that I might make merry with my friends."*

He assumed the way to his father's heart was through correct behavior. When his father greeted his brother with grace, he could not accept it. He assumed his father would disown his brother for wasting his inheritance. He also assumed that His father's acceptance and approval would continue to be his alone. And he considered himself the only good son. His mind was full of rivalry, jealousy, and competition. He had a price tag on all his labor and works. The price tag was that he assumed his actions had won him the place of the favorite son in his father's heart. Assumption, comparison, as well as expectation, are always looking for acceptance and approval from man.

In Luke 2:42–49 we have another example of assumption leading to rejection in the account of the boy Jesus:

> *And when he was twelve years old, they went up to Jerusalem after the custom of the feast. And when they had fulfilled the days, as they returned, the child Jesus tarried behind in Jerusalem; and Joseph and his mother knew not of it. But they, supposing him to have been in the company, [assumption] went a day's journey; and they sought him among their kinfolk and acquaintance. And when they found him not, they turned back again to Jerusalem, seeking him. And it came to pass, that after three days they found him in the temple, sitting in the midst of the doctors, both hearing them, and asking them*

questions. And all that heard him were astonished at his understanding and answers. And when they saw him, they were amazed: and his mother said unto him, 'Son, why hast thou thus dealt with us? [offense] Behold, thy father and I have sought thee sorrowing.' [rejection and depression] And he said unto them, How is it that ye sought me? Wist ye not that I must be about my Father's business?

In verse 44 Jesus' parents assumed he was somewhere in the caravan. The assumption mind trap led them into offense in verse 48 when Mary asked Jesus why he had treated them this way. Every parent can relate to what was going through Mary and Joseph's minds as they anxiously looked for Jesus for three days. They searched frantically for him from the time they knew he was missing until they found him. Then they were relieved but also upset by the ordeal.

In Psalm 19:13 we see a way to avoid this mind trap: *"Keep back thy servant also from presumptuous sins; let them not have dominion over me: then shall I be upright, and I shall be innocent from the great transgression."*

How is this accomplished? We are told in the next verse: *"Let the words of my mouth, and the meditation of my heart, be acceptable in thy sight, O Lord, my strength, and my redeemer."*

Our words set the course, and our thoughts are the battleground. We need to keep our minds on God's Word and not let any lie of the enemy exalt itself over His Word. We need to ask the Holy Spirit to help keep us from presumptuous sins and expose any misleading assumptions in our thinking.

1. Why is assumption dangerous to the unrenewed mind?

   _____

2. In what way does assumption come against the love walk?

   _____

3. How did the older brother get upset in the prodigal son story?

_____

4. Why did Joseph and Mary get upset with Jesus?

_____

CHAPTER 3

Recall

Genesis 9:15; John 14:26; James 1:24–25

The synonyms for *recall* in the thesaurus are "to remember, call back to memory, summon, or recollect." In the dictionary, *recall* is defined as "to bring back to mind or remember; to bring the attention of the mind back to the immediate situation." Our minds have the ability to recall things that happened a few minutes ago, a week ago, or years ago. Recall is the unique ability of the brain to remember what happened in the past. We use the memory part of our brain to recall past events.

Because we all have this special ability to recall past events, these recollections can have a powerful emotional and psychological effect on our thought-life. First, let us look at the positive or right-thinking side of recall in Scripture. These verses show us what God remembers and then what we are to remember. Genesis 9:15 says, *"And I will remember my covenant, which is between me and you and every living creature of all flesh; and the waters shall no more become a flood to destroy all flesh."*

After the flood, God made a covenant with Noah. He promised Noah that never again would waters cover the earth. The sign He gave as a reminder of His promise is the rainbow.

Joseph named his oldest son Manasseh, which meant "made me forget." This meant that God gave Joseph relief by letting him forget all the anguish of his youth and the hurts and losses that he suffered at the hands of his brothers. Instead of letting him recall all the bad times, God wiped the anguish from his memory.

The Scripture verse is in Genesis 41:51: *"And Joseph called the name of the firstborn Manasseh: For God, said he, hath made me forget all my toil, and all my father's house."*

In Exodus 6:5 God remembered His covenant with Israel: *"And I have also heard the groaning of the children of Israel, whom the Egyptians keep in bondage; and I have remembered my covenant."*

Under the Mosaic Law, Israel was to remember the Sabbath day. In Exodus 31:15–17 God speaks His command:

> *Six days may work be done; but in the seventh is The Sabbath of rest, holy to the Lord: whosoever doeth any work in the Sabbath day, he shall surely be put to death. Wherefore the children of Israel shall keep the Sabbath, to observe the Sabbath through-out their generations, for a perpetual covenant. It is a sign between me and the children of Israel forever: for in six days the Lord made heaven and earth, and on the seventh day he rested, and was refreshed.*

Under the Old Covenant, God wanted the people to rest one day out of seven. But we, under the New Covenant can enter into a nonstop, twenty-four-hour-a-day, seven-days-a-week rest! We can stay in this full rest in our spirit and soul even if there are issues that still need to be confronted.

God prepared a physical place for that rest, the land of Canaan, for His people. But the people of Israel did not possess the promised land because of their unbelief. We also have a promised land within our spirit. When we apply the Word of God to our soul it causes our soul to rest. This is the land we are to possess and occupy. Our spirit has been born from above, and Christ is now within us. Our soul can also have the mind of Christ, according to 1 Corinthians 2:16, and the life which is in our spirit can come and take up residence in our body.

Do not recall the hurts, losses, and problems. Recall the benefits of God! Recall the promises that He gave us in His Word. Recall the confidence we felt the last time we entered into a promise with Him. Do not lose out on entering into His rest because of unbelief. Go back to Him and receive it for your present situation.

Several years ago, my daughter called me on the telephone and said, "Mom, I feel so overwhelmed! Do you know how to put down contact paper? I can't get it to lie flat!" She went on to tell me she was overwhelmed with her studies, overwhelmed with her house, and overwhelmed with her contact paper project! I said to her, "First of all, let's deal with the thinking before arriving at being overwhelmed." Because we do things in our own strength and wisdom, many times we take on unnecessary stress, pressure, and tension. When we do not pray about our lives, we can take on the weight of each problem. These problems can add up until we feel under them, carrying their heavy weight. If we know we are susceptible to getting under stress, pressure, and tension, then we must resist them, in Jesus' Name (James 4:7; Philippians 2:9–10). Remember, Jesus' Name has been given to us to use against any other name. By our faith in His name, we can render null and void the stressful power of other names such as contact paper projects, study deadlines, and even housecleaning pressures.

We cannot have a stress-filled, pressure-filled, or tension-filled outlook on any project with a deadline. We cannot allow stress, pressure or mental striving into our thoughts, or we will end up with the thinking of being overwhelmed! My daughter and I prayed and bound the stress, pressure, and tension in her life. We bound the thinking of being overwhelmed and received the peace of God to flood her mind. We committed each project to God and received His wisdom, direction, and success for each in Jesus' Name. She could then take a deep breath and attack each project with confidence God would lead her. Most people keep saying what they think their problem is, but they do not take authority over the spiritual forces that are behind them. It is time to realize the source of the harassment and exercise the authority God gave us! He gave us dominion over everything, except the will of others.

Joshua 1:9 in the Living Bible says, *"Yes, be bold and strong. Banish fear and doubt for remember the Lord your God is with you wherever you go."* This is something for us to remember as believers. He is with us now, wherever we go. He does not want us to walk in fear. Psalm 112:6–7 talks about what to do when fear comes: *Surely he shall not be moved forever. The righteous shall be an everlasting remembrance. He shall not be afraid of evil tidings: his heart is fixed, trusting in the Lord.*

God wants us to be strong in Him. He does not want His children to cower in fear and be moved by every circumstance. This comforting and confidence building verse lets us know that there will be an everlasting remembrance for all of us who are considered righteous before God. And the memory of the just is blessed.

John 14:26 tells the believers: *"But the Comforter, which is the Holy Ghost, whom the Father will send in my name, he shall teach you all things, and bring all things to your remembrance, whatsoever I have said unto you."*

There should be no mental striving, just receive from the Holy Spirit. It is His ministry to bring to our remembrance everything we need to know. It is His ministry to help us recall the things He wants to teach us. I decided and declared that the Holy Spirit would bring all things to my remembrance.

Many times I remembered reading a verse in my Bible, but I did not know where it was. I did not know where to find it but refused to strive in my mind. I would not look it up in a Concordance, and I would not search for it in my Bible. I decided to simply receive the location of the Scripture in my Bible from the Holy Spirit. I waited on Him. I let the Holy Spirit show me where it was, and the way He did it each time was really a blessing. I heard the very verse quoted in a conversation, taught on TV, or written in a book I was reading. This was my experience time and again! I always received the Scripture I had asked the Holy Spirit to bring to my remembrance. He is faithfully on the job and more than ready and willing to do the same for anyone.

When we take communion, it says in 1 Corinthians 11:24–25 that we are to remember that His body was broken and His blood was shed for us. We are to take communion in remembrance of His sacrifice for our sake.

One of the things we need to purpose to do is described in James 1:24–25:

> *For he beholdeth himself, and goeth his way, and straightway forgetteth what manner of man he was. But whoso looketh into the perfect law of liberty, and continueth therein, he being not a forgetful hearer, but a doer of the work, this man shall be blessed in his deed.*

This is vital for someone who wants to live in victory. The victorious life comes by being an effectual doer of the Word. An example of this was when my grown son John fixed his friend's motorcycle. After John had taken out all the dents, they went to the paint booth to spray it. On the way over, his friend prayed that they would have the protection of God and that the motorcycle would look as good as new again. They also prayed that the completed work would satisfy and fulfill his heart's desire.

But when my son got all suited up with the mask on and the paint sprayer in his hand, his friend panicked and said, "Wait! This looks like more than what we should have done. We shouldn't have gotten into such a big job!" His fearful reaction was an example of a person who prayed about a situation but when he got into the heat of it forgot what he prayed. He forgot all the spiritual preparation he had done through his prayers.

This is what the verse in James describes. He forgot to recall *what manner of man he was.* We cannot forget what we have already prayed for and received. We are to use our prayers as anchors to hold us from drifting into doubt. Once we have prayed, received, and said, "Amen," we must walk it all the way through in faith without doubt.

We need the Word imprinted on our minds like they did in the Holy Land and the way devout Jews still do in Israel today. The Word of God is written on a forehead piece that comes down over their eyes so they can literally keep the Word in front of them and meditate on it. When we have received the Word of God on a situation, we need to learn to use our ability of recall to our own advantage. We have to say, "Yes, I agree with this and I will remember this. I want this promise in my life. I want to walk in it." Then we have to stand solid in the perfect law of liberty and continue therein, not forgetting what manner of man we are and what we have prayed and received.

If we are believers, we are believers when life's circumstances are good and we are believers when the pressure of a situation is attacking our minds. Whether we have no conflicts or whether we have many, we must never forget what manner of man we have become in Christ. We must recall the image we received from God through prayer and His Word and hold on to that image in our hearts and minds. As it says in James, we must not walk away after seeing ourselves in the mirror and forget what we looked like! The whole point of receiving from God and standing on His Word is not to do it only when everything is going smoothly but *to believe and keep on receiving* no matter what is happening in our lives. By the way, the motorcycle came out beautifully, and my son John said, "It was the best job he ever did!"

If we do not have the Word of God in readiness and prepared to use it like the sword that it is, we will revert to our old habits of thinking and reacting. We will go back to our old ways of handling situations. These old ways may include turning on the television and escaping or it may be going to bed and sleeping for a while. When we revert to our old ways, we are not making God and His Word the source of our strength. We must start fighting in the spirit by using the words we have received from the Word! This is how to engage the enemy in spiritual warfare.

According to the Bible, the prince of the air, the god of this world, and the world system have already been defeated. Jesus has already paid the price for victory over them all. According to the Word, they really have no hold on us anymore, even if we think they do! And again, it is the devil deceiving us. We just think all this stuff coming at us is real and that it has so much power over us that we must be defeated. Why don't we just say instead, "I have power and authority over the devil in this situation, in the Name of Jesus!"

Philippians 3:13 says: *"Brethren, I count not myself to have apprehended: but this one thing I do, forgetting those things which are behind, and reaching forth to those things which are before."*

In this verse, Paul tells us that recalling the past can hinder us from going on with the Lord. On the negative or wrong-thinking side of recall is the person who is not forgetting those things that are behind, things that happened in the past. The voice of *recall* mind trap always has regrets. It says, "If only I would have said this . . .," or "I should have done that . . ." If the enemy can keep us stuck in the past, he can render us powerless today.

A good example of this is seen in the book of Exodus. Chapters 2, 3, 16, 17, and 18 gives an account of the children of Israel's exodus from Egypt. It shows how they continued to murmur in the wilderness in spite of everything God had done for them. In these chapters, God delivered the children of Israel out of Egypt with miraculous signs and wonders. God fed the children of Israel in the wilderness with supernatural food called *manna*. He made water spring out from a rock at Horeb to quench their thirst. He also sent them a cloud to guide them by day and a pillar of fire by night. He cared for their every need for forty years.

With God's good care, their clothes and shoes did not wear out and their bodies were kept strong and healthy. God did all these things for them, as well as leading them to the land of plenty that they would be able to call their own. Yet, instead of being grateful for and content with what they had, thoughts of *recall* crept into their minds. They recalled all the things they had in Egypt—the meat, the onions, the garlic, and the leeks. They missed the variety of the food and the wine. They wandered through the desert, camping in tents, and missed their houses in Egypt. They began to live in the past and regret what they had lost to such an extent that they became blind to what God was doing for them in the present.

They forgot to recall the grueling work, the cruel slavery, and the excessive abuse from their Egyptian taskmasters! They only remembered what the devil wanted them to remember. This mind trap only recalls what best suits the devil's purposes. This blinds us from seeing God's current provisions for us. The abuses and beatings the children of Israel suffered at the hands of the Egyptians were forgotten. The humiliation of slavery and the backbreaking labor they had to do was also forgotten.

Only the attractive things about Egypt were remembered, mainly the spicy foods that filled their bellies! The Israelites were so defeated by this mind trap that they wandered for forty years in a twenty-mile stretch of desert between Egypt and the land of Canaan. They were stuck in no-man's land for forty years because of their bitter attitude toward God. They were unable to take the land and move into the promises of God because of the recall mind trap and their unbelief.

In Exodus chapter 16, we read the actual statements of the children of Israel, and we can hear their attitude in their words. We can hear rejection speaking. They moved from recall to offense and then into rejection. Through their murmurings and grumbling, they were expressing their anger and offense. They were angry with Moses and Aaron for bringing them out of Egypt. But they were really angry at God. This is their rejection statement in Exodus 16:2–3:

> *And the whole congregation of the children of Israel murmured against Moses and Aaron in the wilderness: And the children of Israel said to them, Would to God we had died by the hand of the Lord in the land of Egypt, when we sat by the flesh pots, and when we did eat bread to the full, for ye have brought us forth into this wilderness, to kill this whole assembly with hunger.*

This is why Paul says in Philippians 3:13 that we have to forget those things that are behind in order to go forward. I have seen that recalling the *things which are behind* can prevent marriages from being reconciled in the present. I have seen how *recall* can keep family members locked into thinking condemning and negative thoughts about a young couple's poor judgment or past mistakes. The family's attitude is locked into that one past mistake and keeps them from releasing the couple to grow and change.

In one case, the husband committed adultery and told his wife about it. Even though she forgave him, she was still plagued by the memory recall of the past event. As she allowed her mind to be consumed by her husband's past failure, she created a wall of grievance that served as an obstacle and prevented reconciliation with him in the present. It also robbed them of their future happiness together. She was having a hard time entering into her marriage because of her constant plaguing thoughts. These thoughts were a source of harassment and mental trauma to her every time she recalled what had transpired between her husband and the other woman. For those with high imaginations, being told the details only gives them more fuel for recall.

The wife of the husband needed to cast down the recalling image of her husband's adulterous act. It was exalting itself against the provisions of God. Be on guard. Be obedient. Keep your thought-life on the Word. There must be a decision to not allow our minds to play with recall. It is a very dangerous mind trap.

The rewards for obedience in this case were a recovered marriage and fulfillment for both partners. The wife experienced the reality of Philippians 3:13–14:

> *Brethren, I count not myself to have apprehended:*
> *but this one thing I do, forgetting those things which*
> *are behind, and reaching forth to those things which*
> *are before, I press toward the mark for the prize of*
> *the high calling of God in Christ Jesus.*

She used this verse to put an end to her harassing thoughts and found the ability to enter into the present blessings of their relationship.

Lot's wife in the Old Testament was told not to look back when they were leaving Sodom and Gomorrah, but she did. She looked back at what she was leaving and was turned into a pillar of salt. If we look back, we will never grow. If we disobey, we will never grow.

She never grew into the things God had prepared for her. She became a pillar of salt. Lot's wife is a picture of salt's powers of preservation. She stayed the same and never grew or changed. As a result, her fate was solidification and she died from disobeying God. God does not want our recalling thoughts to get us stuck solid like Lot's wife. He wants us to grow and change and break free from the past.

When Dennis and I came back into our marriage after a nine-month separation, we made an agreement with each other never to bring up the past. We both acknowledged the pain we had inflicted upon each other and apologized for the pain we caused one another. The best way for us to accept the healing that God was performing in our marriage was not to dwell on the deceits and hurts of the past. God wanted us to reach forth for the good things which were before us. In doing so, we had to guard our minds against recall as often as it came up. It was the only way for us to survive and have a future together.

1. What is the best way for us to forget the negative part of the past?

   _____

2. What happens to us when we bring the negative part of the past into the now?

   _____

3. Why does the enemy of our mind want us to stay in the past?

   _____

4. What does one have to become to live in victory?

   _____

5. Whose ministry is it to bring to our remembrance the Word of God?

_____

6. How can recall be an enemy of faith?

_____

7. When is recall an asset to our faith?

_____

CHAPTER 4

Projecting

Romans 8:3; 1 Corinthians 10:13; Ephesians 4:27

On the flip side of *recall* is *projecting*. In the thesaurus, the synonyms for *projecting* are "a goal, a plan, an aim, an intention or an undertaking." Projecting is a predetermined plan that the mind contemplates. The dictionary says *projecting* is "to send forth in one's thoughts; to project oneself into the future; to externalize a thought or a feeling so that it appears to have subjective reality."

Projecting makes a thought or situation so subjective and real to us that even if it is only imagined or mentally fabricated, we are convinced it is real. Projecting makes it real to us today, even though it is a situation that has not even taken place yet. The thoughts our mind entertains and projects today may or may not actually take place in the future.

Let's look at the positive or right-thinking side of projecting first. The concept of a plan is the one most frequently seen in the Bible. The implication in Psalm 119:37 is, *Turn me away from wanting any other plan than Yours. Revive my heart toward You.* Verse 130 goes on to imply: *As Your plan unfolds even the simple can understand it.*

In Acts 2:23 Peter says, *"But God, following His predetermined plan, let you use the Roman government to nail Him to the cross and murder Him."* Peter was talking to the crowd on the day of Pentecost, after the baptism of the Holy Spirit had been given. These are examples of God's projections or plans for us and for our future. God had a predetermined plan for all of us to receive salvation.

In Romans 8:3 we read:

> *For what the law could not do, in that it was weak through the flesh, God sending his own Son in the likeness of sinful flesh, and for sin, condemned sin in the flesh: That the righteousness of the law might be fulfilled in us, who walk not after the flesh, but after the Spirit.*

We are not saved from sin's grasp by knowing the Law or the commandments of God. We cannot and we do not keep them, but God put into effect a predetermined plan to save us. Thank God! He sent His Own Son in human form to save us. His body was just like ours, except that our bodies are sinful and His knew no sin. He destroyed sin's control over us by giving Himself as a sacrifice for sin. God began His predetermined plan from the foundations of the earth, and He stayed with the plan until the fullness of time when Jesus came, as He was prophesied to come through the prophets. We have His plan, and we are still walking out the plan He has for each one of us. He has plans for us individually, as well as a plan for our entire family. His plan is for our whole family to live in eternity with Him.

The negative or wrong-thinking side of projecting is when someone makes a plan and decides that if it is not going to work out the way they thought it should, then they will get hurt or they will fail. This is when they fall into the projecting mind trap. Moses experienced the battle with projecting in Exodus chapter 3 and 4 when he was tending his flock. One day he came upon a burning bush. Strangely enough, even though the bush was burning, it was not consumed by the fire. Then the voice of God spoke to him from the bush. He told Moses to go to Egypt and deliver the Israelites.

God promised to be with him, provide him with the words to say to Pharaoh, and assured him that even the elders would listen to him. God promised Moses that He would do miraculous signs and wonders through him, and not only would the Israelites be delivered, but they would also plunder the Egyptians of much material treasures when they left the country.

After all these promises, Moses said, "But behold, they will not believe me nor hearken unto my voice. For they will say the Lord has not appeared unto me." In this case, Moses was projecting failure for himself even before he set out. He did not feel up to the mission even though God briefed him of all his accomplishments and successes ahead of time. The enemy kept him focused on his own natural abilities or lack of them, and he was using Moses's negative projecting to keep him from doing God's will.

In 1 Corinthians 10:13 in the New American Standard Bible, we read:

> *There hath no temptation taken you but such as is common to man: but God is faithful, who will not allow you to be tempted above that you are able; but will with the temptation also make a way to escape, that you may be able to bear it.*

The devil brings temptations into our everyday circumstances of life. When we allow our eyes to focus on the natural, on what is happening to us, we will feel helpless and become hopeless. When we do not have the spiritual ability or maturity to conquer the situation, God is faithful to give us a way of escape.

Dennis and I received a wonderful way of escape when we moved from Illinois to California. God gave us some powerful supernatural experiences with Him, but because we lacked the knowledge and understanding of His Word, we were defenseless in ourselves. The temptations we had just come out of in Illinois would have overtaken us again had God not been faithful and seen us through.

On the other hand, Moses did not receive a way of escape. God specifically told him His plan. He had the opportunity to believe

God's words or look at the circumstances. We will not see God's ability working for us until we put forth faith, based on a particular knowledge of His will.

Another example of projecting is found in Numbers chapter 13:26 through chapter 14:5. This passage describes what the spies saw in the land of Canaan.

In verses 31-33 we read:

> *"But the men that went up with him said, We be not able to go up against the people for they are stronger than we And they brought up an evil report of the land which they had searched, unto the children of Israel."*

Earlier in this passage, it describes what the ten spies saw in the land of Canaan. They perceived the strength of the people in the land, and they formed a negative report in their minds. Of the twelve spies only Joshua and Caleb gave a positive report of the situation. The other ten saw themselves as grasshoppers in their own sight. They saw themselves not equal to the task and no match for the inhabitants of the land. They projected that the men of Canaan also saw them as grasshoppers! Verse 33 says, *"And we were in our own sight as grasshoppers and so we were in their sight."* With negative projecting, they already saw their own inadequacies, no capabilities, and failure. Their mission was doomed from the start in their own minds.

After the people heard the report of the ten spies, they too got stuck in projection. They also became offended at the whole situation because they projected future failure if they went into the land. They felt rejected by God and went into fear and unbelief. They were in so much fear and unbelief and mental striving with the whole situation that there was no talking to them. They wanted to choose another leader and go back to Egypt. Then Moses and Aaron fell on their faces before all the assembly of the congregation of the children of Israel. Joshua and Caleb, who had also spied out the land, tore their clothes in desperation and gave their account of the land to dispel the evil report of the other ten spies who had projected negatively. However, there was no turning their unbelief and fear.

When I was in college, I heard many of my classmates projecting and expressing their future failures. This is what happened to a young man who was in one of my classes and was caught by the mind trap of projecting. We had a term paper due, and he said, "I know the professor is not going to like my term paper. He never likes anything I turn in! I don't know why I even bother to go to school." By taking this attitude, he already failed the class in his mind and his projecting came true when he later dropped the class before he had to hand in his term paper. He projected his fear of failure, and it actually materialized.

Another example of projecting that I heard while in school was usually expressed after an exam. The students made negative projections about their test results and would experience anxiety and defeat until the grades were posted or handed out. They projected these negative feelings without having all the facts. By doing this, they lost their peace of mind while they waited. They started going from projecting into offense and from offense into rejection and then into depression.

In both these cases, the students had taken negative projecting thoughts to be theirs instead of taking authority over them. It takes a disciplined mind with renewed thinking to recognize that many times our thoughts are not coming from inside of us. Rather, some are coming directly as suggestions from the devil to see which ones can find a home in our thinking. There is a popular saying, "You can let the birds fly over your head, but you don't have to let them make a nest in your hair!" The suggestions come at us from the devil to see which ones we will let in. When we play around with thoughts and give them a place in our minds, we are giving place to the enemy.

In Ephesians 4:27 God says, *"Neither give place to the devil."* This verse tells us we have a choice which thoughts we let in and which thoughts we reject. We must be watchful and on guard to not allow our minds to dwell on any thoughts that work against us.

Do our thoughts line up with what the Word of God says? Do our thoughts reflect God's desire for our lives? Do our thoughts instill faith? Do our thoughts exalt the Name of Jesus? We can develop our own biblical yardstick for discerning our own thoughts. When the mind trap of projecting speaks, we need to resist the thought and come back at it with the Word of God and by faith send the truth found in God's Word into our future instead of negative projections. This will dispel the lies of the enemy.

If the devil speaks of our impending financial doom, we can quote him Philippians 4:19, "But my God shall supply all my needs according to His riches in glory by Christ Jesus." If fear of failure arises because of some future event, we can think on Philippians 4:13, "I can do all things through Christ who strengthens me." We can make plans for the future based on God's Word and His will for our lives.

Whenever we see failure coming our way or know that we are incapable of doing something in ourselves, we can always go to God and get His strength for it! We cannot be passive. There is no such thing as being passive and saying within ourselves, *Okay, I know this is self-unacceptance* or *This sounds like I have an expectation on this person or situation.* We cannot passively think these things and do nothing about them. We have to resist them. We have to take hold of them and say, "No! You are not part of my thinking!" What we all want to do is say, "Oh, I'm so tired of it all!" What we are really saying is, "I'm going to be passive. I'm not going to fight. I'm just going to lie down under this and wait for it to go away."

I caught myself doing this—actually, I did it for weeks! I was still functioning to a degree but was in a mild form of depression. I was hopeless about my whole life and thought, *Why bother anyway?* When I came out of that depression and got back into faith, I said, "Why don't you practice what you preach?" I realized I had to do in my life what I was telling others to do. I needed to practice what I was preaching! In order to confound the enemy, I had to receive from God what He already promised was mine and change my thinking, speaking, and actions.

A third example of projecting is when projection hinders future plans because of its negative impact on the people's thinking who are involved. When someone bases their future plans on projecting negatively, it is projecting failure before they are even there. An example of this is in the case of a young man who went into a relationship with a girl and projected into the future how their relationship would turn out.

He thought to himself, *If we're going to have this relationship, she's going to have to be prepared to support me for three years while I go to school.* He projected or put forth the image of her taking care of him and bringing in the finances while he was finishing school. When he stated his plans to her, she had to decide whether she wanted to support him and still have a relationship with him or not. He was projecting his plans into the future and making her a part of his projection. By the time he shared the only way he could see for them to have a future, he was all the way into depression. Projecting locked him into seeing only one solution, that of her supporting him. Projecting had caused him to lose the possibilities of today. He could not see any other options for them, and he had no faith to receive any other way.

The way for this couple to avoid projecting was for them to pray about their future and together put forth a plan with more possibilities for success without the finances being the center of the pressure. During their prayer time, the young man realized that a new option for him was to take fewer classes and find a part-time job. The burden did not need to be carried entirely by his girlfriend. It was too great for her, and she could easily fall into resentment. This new option would mean that it would take longer for him to complete his education, but this way each party would bear responsibility, and they could go forward helping each other prepare for their future together.

As we read the Old Testament, we see the nation of Israel was never satisfied. Anytime they looked at their situation in the natural, they wanted things to be better. They wanted something more than what they had. They wanted to be like their surrounding nations who had kings ruling over them. Yet God called them to be separate, and God calls us to be separate. The problem is we have another whole mentality that we live by. The nation of Israel went back to idolatry, and they murmured constantly against their lot in life. Likewise, when we get in the flesh and look at things in the natural realm, we do the same thing.

We do not want to live by faith. We get mad, and we do not want to resist anymore. We want to give in (Hebrews 11:6), and yet we cannot. There is no way for us to live except to live by faith because as soon as we are not living by faith, the devil has us! If we say, "Oh well, I'm just going to take it easy for a while." The devil's got us just by taking on this thinking! There is no such thing as indecision. Indecision is a decision to not decide on something. If we say, "I'm just not going to deal with it," that is a decision in itself!

We may think we can put the whole thing on hold, but we are mistaken. We must be proactive and not passive; otherwise, we will sink into unbelief. Unbelief and idolatry were the nation of Israel's two biggest sins. After idolatry, the natural progression is whoring around, which God calls adultery. As soon as we have an idol in front of us, that is exactly what we are doing—committing spiritual adultery. When we turn from God to idols, we break the first commandment that says, *You shall not have any other gods before Me.*

The underlying force that is the opposite of faith is fear, and that is the ingredient the devil needs in order to start his operations. If we take his thought process and allow fear to take hold of us, it will take us over. Helplessness, hopelessness, and powerlessness have an element of fear in them because we look at the picture and feel trapped and overwhelmed. There appears to be no way out, and this produces fear. If we say we are tired and we do not want to deal with anything anymore, we are actually being passive. If we are murmuring and are in fear, we are going to go around the mountain we created for ourselves again! Whatever our problem is, we will see it loom larger than it really is and it will feel impossible to overcome because our attitude is wrong. We are not going to conquer it until we go from fear to faith in our thinking. The same things will come at us over and over again. We have been given the ability to conquer it. Remember, when we turn to the Word, we will always find a way of successful escape!

1. Why is projection an enemy of faith?

    _____

2. What is God's plan for us in this life?

    _____

3. When did Moses go wrong in his fight with Pharaoh and the Egyptians?

    _____

4. What did the ten spies see, and where did they see it?

    _____

5. What will God do for us when we turn to Him in tough situations?

    _____

6. How do we combat negative thoughts before we get to the end result?

    _____

7. When should we judge the thoughts we get in our minds?

    _____

8. What should we do when we recognize a negative projection in our minds?

    _____

Comparison

2 Corinthians 3:18; Galatians 6:14

The synonyms in the thesaurus for *comparison* are "to contrast, to parallel, an association, correlation, resemblance or similarity." The closest word to *comparison* in the Bible is the word *likeness*. The dictionary defines *compare* as "to notice or point out the likenesses or differences of anything; to liken or contrast."

In order to avoid the wrong thinking of the mind trap of comparison, we need to be established in right-thinking. There are many right-thinking examples in the Bible. We can start with the fact that we are made in the *likeness of God* according to Genesis 1:26-27:

> *And God said, Let us make man in our image, after our likeness: and let them have dominion over the fish of the sea, and over the fowl of the air, and over the cattle, and over all the earth and over every creeping thing that creepeth upon the earth. So God created man in his own image, in the image of God created he him; male and female created he them.*

From this Scripture, we see that we are made in His image and we must remember God does not make junk! We are totally acceptable to Him. According to Romans 8:16–17, we are the children of God and joint heirs with Christ. As God's children, we occupy a close and loving position in His Kingdom, and as joint heirs with Christ, we will inherit the blessings of eternal life and the power to become *more than conquerors* in this life.

The Bible is full of Scriptures that build our confidence in God. We can look to Him for our similarities as we identify with Christ. Second Corinthians 3:18 is a good example: *"And we, who with unveiled faces all reflect the Lord's glory, are being transformed into his likeness with ever-increasing glory, which comes from the Lord, who is the Spirit."*

In the ancient Bible lands, the women wore veils to cover their faces. No one could look at their faces except their husbands and close family members. Unveiled faces talks about the intimate relationship we have in God's family. We reflect the Lord's glory with unveiled faces. As long as we continue to transform our thinking and identify with Christ's redemption, we take on His characteristics and increase in glory. This is God's presence and power working through us. We are new creations of righteousness, and we have a new identity in Christ.

There is a beautiful picture in Isaiah 40:31 that shares instructions on what to do when we feel weary. It reads: *"But they that wait upon the Lord shall renew their strength; they shall mount up with wings as eagles; they shall run, and not be weary; and they shall walk, and not faint."*

The instructions are to wait on the Lord or minister to the Lord, and our strength will be renewed. Eagles have notches in their wings that allow them to be locked in flight. This gives them the ability to soar above the clouds and stay in this position for long periods of time without growing weary. They can hover and glide effortlessly on the wind. This picture of the eagle helps me to hold on to God and stay high above each and every circumstance that doesn't line up with God's best for me.

When we come out of or mentally leave our identification with Christ, we come down to where we see only the information in the natural realm. This is when the comparison mind trap influences our thinking. It is said that our brains operate on a mismatch system. The human brain can see what is wrong with something before it sees what is right. We are always ready to compare the differences or similarities between us and someone else. We then judge our own value based on these differences or similarities. It is usually a no-win situation. If we come out beneath the other person, we feel miserable; if we come out on top, we fall into pride.

Sibling rivalry is a classic example of comparison at work. Cain and Abel got stuck in this mind trap in Genesis 4:3-5:

> *And in the process of time it came to pass, that Cain brought of the fruit of the ground an offering unto the Lord. And Abel, he also brought of the firstlings of his flock and of the fat thereof. And the Lord had respect unto Abel and to his offering: But unto Cain and to his offering he had not respect. And Cain was very wroth, and his countenance fell.*

Cain's offering was not accepted by God; therefore, he got upset. God encouraged him to take stock of himself and make some changes. Verse 7 says, *"If thou doest well, shalt thou not be accepted?"* Yet by this time, Cain was entangled in the comparison mind trap. Cain compared himself to Abel, whose offering God received, and he became enraged.

How many times do we think our problems are someone else's fault? This was the outcome in verse 8: *"And Cain talked with Abel, his brother: and it came to pass, when they were in the field, that Cain rose up against Abel his brother, and slew him."*

Comparing ourselves with others sidetracks us from the real issues. It can also defeat us before we even get started. I have seen many Christians who doubted the reality of their salvation because it was not as dramatic as some conversion experiences. Because they compared their experiences with that of others, they gave up spiritually and lived in varying degrees of depression. In Galatians 6:4 Paul tells us, *"But let every man prove his own work, and then he shall have rejoicing in himself alone, and not in another."* The *New International Version* of Galatians 6:4 says, *"Then he can take pride in himself, without comparing himself to somebody else."*

Early in our Christian walk, Dennis and I realized from Ephesians 6:9 that *"God is not a respecter of persons."* We went to praise and worship services and heard others praying the most wonderful prayers and saw them move in the things of the Spirit. But rather than get discouraged or upset, we decided to go for God's best. Instead of comparing what they did to what we could do, we focused on God. If we saw someone walking in the abilities of God that were above and beyond ours, we chose not to get discouraged or upset, but saw that it was also available to us. We chose to see the accomplishments of others as a way to encourage ourselves that we could also attain what they had already attained.

When we stay out of comparison, we can appreciate our brothers and sisters in the body of Christ and see that all of us are on this journey together. We may be in different places in our walks, but we are one body. There is no place for comparison in the body of Christ.

In order for two things to be compared, they must be separate entities, but the Bible tells us in 1 Corinthians 12:12 that *"We are one body."* The enemy uses comparison to create factions within the church to provoke us to battle among ourselves. In 1 Corinthians 1:10–31, Paul confronts this problem. He tells us that believers in the church at Corinth were dividing themselves into factions, each standing behind a different apostle. He asks a poignant question in verse 1, *"Is Christ divided?"* Then in chapter 12:14–20 he illustrates the absurdity of comparison within the church:

> *For the body is not one member, but many. If the foot shall say, because I am not the hand, I am not of the body; is it therefore not of the body? And if the ear shall say, because I am not the eye, I am not of the body; is it therefore not of the body? If the whole body were an eye, where were the hearing? If the*

whole body were hearing, where were the smelling?
But now God hath set the members everyone of them
in the body, as it hath pleased Him. And if they were
all one member, where were the body? But now are
they many members, yet but one body.

Comparison is a mind trap that individuals can fall into, and it can happen on a larger scale when one church compares itself to another. Comparing ourselves to another believer is just as damaging as comparing one church to another. Each has its place in the body of Christ and has its own unique function. We cannot all be the same. This is one of the enemy's most effective tools to divide Christians.

A friend of mine shared a comparison mind trap example with me. She saw this take place at her church when the new pastor came and replaced the previous pastor (an older man). Since coming to her church, the young pastor and his wife had made many friendships with people their own age, but some of the older members of the congregation fell into the comparison mind trap. They started comparing the way the new pastor made friendships with younger couples and not with older ones. They became angry with him and said he was causing hard feelings among them. They spread anger and rejection all over the congregation and blamed him for neglecting the older couples, not realizing that the problem first started with their own comparison thinking.

As I said before, comparison thinking forces us into thinking that we are either higher or lower than the person we are comparing ourselves with and both are no-win situations. In this case, the older members of the congregation missed their senior pastor's friendship. Instead of realizing that each generation naturally gravitates to its own age group because of common interests, they were comparing how the new pastor treated them. They envied the younger people in the congregation because of how he treated them, and they were upset because they found themselves at the bottom of the totem pole! In this mind trap, the underlying motive of the heart is again looking for acceptance and approval from man instead of receiving from Christ the acceptance we already have in Him.

The mind trap of comparison also leads us down the path to being offended, rejected, and depressed. Jealousy is included in comparison thinking and is the basis for much sibling rivalry. If we entertain comparison in our thinking, it will not stay in one area. Before we know it, we will be looking through the eyes of anger at everything in our lives and we will say that nobody notices us or cares how we feel about anything. Then the thinking will escalate to "Everything I do always turns out wrong. I am just a failure and what is the use anyway?" This thinking is one of the characteristics of depression. At some point, we need to trace back in our thinking patterns and ask ourselves, "How did I get here?" We will not find our answer by pointing a finger and saying, "They did this to me." That is resorting to blame. The Holy Spirit will show us this mind trap, if we ask Him.

Remember, it was something we did in our thinking that put us into offense, rejection, or depression. This is vital for us to realize and remember when we find ourselves in these emotional places. There are too many people trapped in offense, rejection, and depression because they do not know how they got there and how to get out. Not only do we need to learn to reverse our thinking patterns, but also share with others how to reverse their thinking as well. This will help us all to expose depression and give us alternate thinking habits. We have to stop allowing mind traps to take us on these no-win trips into depression.

1. How does the enemy use comparison in the church?

   _____

2. What is his purpose?

   _____

3. What does comparison thinking force us to do?

   _____

4.   What is the underlying motive of the heart in comparison?

_____

5.   What part does jealousy play in comparison thinking?

_____

6.   In whose mind are we always accepted?

_____

7.   What do we do when we feel weary?

_____

8.   Why does the enemy want us to look or compare ourselves with others?

_____

9.   What is the real benefit to staying out of comparison?

_____

CHAPTER 6

Intellectualizing

2 Corinthians 3:16; Hebrews 4:12; Philippians 1:6

In the thesaurus, the synonyms for the word *intellectual* are "academic, genius, thinker, educated, intelligent, learned, philosophical, rational, reasoner, and scholar." The dictionary says an *intellectual* has "a devotion to intellectual pursuit; believes the doctrine that knowledge comes wholly from pure reason, and believes in logic or rationalism without aid from the senses." In the Bible, *intellectualizing* is recorded as "the act of reasoning, and to reason things through." When a person has pride in intellectual knowledge they may have a hard time hearing about the things of God. When people are into intellectualizing, it could become a form of bondage to them.

When we fall into the trap of intellectualizing, we rely exclusively on our own brain power based on our senses and ignore the counsel of the Holy Spirit. Many of us do this without even realizing it. Young Christians especially fall into this trap. Thus far, they have always relied on their own abilities to think things through, and they have not yet learned to hear the Spirit of God. They do not recognize the need to renew their minds with the Word and replace their thoughts with His thoughts.

This is a natural phase that each born-again believer passes through, like a child passes through the teething or toddler stage in human development. The key, however, is to pass through and not stay in this phase. The devil would like nothing better than to keep Christians as immature babies for the rest of their Christian walk (1 Corinthians 3:2)!

We might think that academic types are most prone to this trap, but that is not always true. People who have a low estimation of their own mental capacities fall prey to this mind trap, too. They say things like, "I've never been a reader. I will not read the Bible because I can't understand it. I just can't concentrate long enough to get anything out of it!" So they let their Bibles gather dust on the shelf and continue to rely on themselves to get through life. They close God out of their lives by taking defeat in this area instead of stepping out in faith.

A famous man of God did not learn to read until he was an adult. His wife used the Bible to teach him to read and that was the only book he ever read. Several times Bible scholars approached him after hearing him speak because they were amazed at his ability to extract truth from the Word. They thought such knowledge could only be revealed to those who had studied the text in the original language. This man of God relied only upon the Holy Spirit to be his teacher and guide into all truth as stated in (John 16:13). His wisdom and knowledge astonished and amazed the learned Bible scholars of his day.

Another dimension of the mind trap of intellectualizing is that it can also snare a person who knows the Word of God quite well. This is a subtler trick of the enemy and unfortunately often difficult for the person involved to detect. In this form of intellectualizing, the person can read, study, and quote the Word of God but the words do not come alive and penetrate into their soul and spirit. This way, it remains unfruitful in their life. The person who intellectualizes may know the words in their mind, but they remain only facts on the surface of their mind as something outside of their experience. Not until they realize that the written words they are reading can become the spoken Word of God to them, do they make the connection. When they experience the reality that this is God speaking to them personally, then what God said through the Holy Spirit can be applied to their everyday life.

In 2 Corinthians 3:6 Paul says, *"Who also hath made us able ministers of the new testament: not of the letter but of the spirit: for the letter killeth, but the spirit giveth life."* The Pharisees and the Sadducees went by the letter of the law. They constantly quoted the Word of God, but we know their hearts were cold toward God and far from Him or they would have recognized His Son. Jesus said they were like whitewashed tombs. A tomb may look clean and beautiful on the outside, but it is full of death and decay on the inside. We need to rely on the Holy Spirit when we read the Word of God. The Bible is not just literature, as many liberal-minded people would have us believe, but it is a spiritual document that is endowed with spiritual power.

Hebrews 4:12–13 says:

> *The Word of God is quick and powerful and sharper than any two-edged sword, piercing even to the dividing asunder of soul and spirit and the joints and marrow and is a discerner of the thoughts and intents of the heart. Neither is there any creature that is not manifest in his sight: but all things are naked and opened unto the eyes of him with whom we have to do.*

I have come to believe that my intent in life is to yield my will to the Holy Spirit in order to have my reactions, my attitudes, and my way of thinking conform to the will of God through His Word. When it comes to getting revelation knowledge, growing up, changing my attitudes, and increasing in the things of God in my life, I need to stay in the Word and do my best to enter into the rest of God described in Hebrews 4. It is the place where I cease to strive with the spiritual growth for my life. Philippians 1:6 gives me the assurance that I can trust in God's plan for me: *"Being confident in this very thing that He which hath begun a good work in you will perform it until the day of Jesus Christ."*

I have always seen this *good work* to be the powerful Word of God that was started in me. It will conform me to the image of God. It is my purpose not to hinder or stop the development of the Word in my mind.

By bringing salvation or any of the other blessings of God to someone, we are a seed planter. We can plant the seed of the Gospel or be the one who waters or even harvests it, but God brings the increase. We cannot bring the increase. God must do it. We become a co-laborer with Him when we accept His input. It is important for us to keep listening to our teacher, the Holy Spirit, who brings us the truth in every situation. Likewise, we need to listen to Jesus, who is the head of the church and to whom we have committed all the days of our lives. We can effectively function in His body by serving the Father just as Jesus did when He was on the earth. As he said in John 14:10, *"Believest thou not that I am in the Father, and the Father in me? The words that I speak unto you I speak not of myself: but the Father that dwelleth in me, he doeth the works."*

Christians who have not entered the rest of God are always trying to grow themselves up by their own efforts. They are bombarded by obligations and constantly striving to improve themselves. They have spiritual truth right in front of them, but they do not have the revealed knowledge in their hearts to turn that truth into their own experience. Most of the time in these Christians, the missing ingredient is a reverence for God. Instead of relying on God, they rely on their own intellectual abilities.

Revelation knowledge comes from the Holy Spirit into our hearts to meet our needs, solve our problems, and give us insight into spiritual principles that can apply to our lives. This is the deeper way of reading the Bible, when the Holy Spirit reveals Himself to us, instead of just reading and understanding written words with the natural mind.

An example of Scripture that relates the right thinking or positive side of *intellectualizing* is found in Isaiah 1:18: *"Come now, and let us reason together, saith the Lord: though your sins be as scarlet, they shall be as white as snow; though they be red like crimson, they shall be as wool."*

God calls us not to reason with our intellect, nor to reason about our situations, but to reason with Him and get His perspective on our circumstances. Since we have the *Spirit of Truth* inside of us, we need to go directly to the Holy Spirit and reason things through with Him. We need to tap into Him as the valuable resource that He is to us. This is the difference between mental striving and relying on the Holy Spirit to bring the wisdom and knowledge to make a concrete decision.

There have been times in my life, especially when teaching a class, that my beliefs were challenged and I had to go back to square one and ask myself, "Why do I believe this?" Each time, when I searched for answers to why I believed in God and who He was to me or any other doctrinal position I held, I always had to go back to Him. Each time I reasoned things out with Him, He gave me the answer I needed. I concluded, "This is why I believe this, whether it's countered by other people or not."

Each time I had to figure out my beliefs, I grew more secure and stronger in Him than I was before. But I went to God and reasoned everything through with Him! This is the only safe reasoning. He helped me get through the process, and it strengthened me every time I did it.

Paul reasoned with the God-fearing Greeks and turned a considerable number of them from their idols made with man's hands to the true and living God. He tried to persuade the Jews in the synagogues by proclaiming Jesus as the Son of God. He used reason to discuss righteousness and self-control and the future judgment to come to Felix when he was giving him his testimony of who God was to him. Paul used Abraham as an example of a giant of faith in Hebrews 11:19 when he reasoned that because God was a God who raised the dead, Abraham could put his long-awaited and beloved son Isaac on the sacrificial altar. God had promised Abraham that through his seed, Isaac, his descendants would be named and a nation would be called out. He was obedient to God's instructions because he knew God could raise Isaac up from the dead again if necessary. He had complete confidence and faith in God.

On the wrong thinking or negative side of intellectualizing, we have the scribes and Pharisees constantly reasoning among themselves and trying to trap Jesus with their questions. But whatever they were thinking and reasoning in their hearts, Jesus already knew their thoughts. In Luke 15:1–2 their offense is noted as Jesus crosses their lines of religion and tradition: *"Then drew near unto him all the publicans and sinners for to hear him. And the Pharisees and scribes murmured, saying, This man receiveth sinners, and eateth with them."*

Jesus rebukes the scribes and Pharisees in Mark 7:1–9, 13:

> *"Then came together unto him the Pharisees, and certain of the scribes, which came from Jerusalem. And when they saw some of his disciples eat bread with defiled, that is to say, with unwashen hands, they found fault. For the Pharisees, and all the Jews, except they wash their hands oft, eat not, holding the tradition of the elders. And when they come from the market, except they wash, they eat not. And many other things there be, which they have received to hold, as the washing of cups, and pots, brazen vessels, and of tables. Then the Pharisees and scribes asked him, Why, walk not thy disciples according to the tradition of the elders, but eat bread with unwashen hands? He answered and said unto them, Well hath Esaias prophesied of you hypocrites, as it is written, This people honoureth me with their lips, but their heart is far from me. Howbeit in vain do they worship me, teaching for doctrines the commandments of men. For laying aside the commandment of God ye hold the tradition of men as the washing of pots and cups: and any other such like things ye do. And he said unto them, Full well ye reject the commandment of God, that ye may keep your own tradition . . .Making the word of God of*

none effect through your tradition, which ye have delivered: and many such like things do ye."

The Pharisees were constantly offended with Jesus because He would not honor their many laws and rituals. They were threatened by everything He said and did. Jesus caught them doing the letter of the law but ignoring the spirit of the law. They were trying to achieve God's favor by their works. Jesus came to show them the love of God, but they could not grasp it because their intellect was focused on and consumed by doing the letter of the law.

A number of years ago I made a commitment to change. I purposed in my heart that if there was a new way God was moving in my life or in the lives of those around me, I would change my present point of view to stay current with His move. I do not ever want any hidden traditions hindering my flowing with God. I do not want to be performing the letter of the law like the Pharisees and miss the spirit of the law. I refuse to be in a rut with God and miss His move in the church. The Pharisees were so encumbered about with all their laws and traditions that they missed Jesus. He was right there with them, but they missed Him. They were too busy being critical of outward ways of doing things, and we often fall into the same trap today.

1. Who do we ignore when we rely on our senses for our answers?

2. What is the Holy Spirit's ministry in us?

3. What is the fruit of intellectualizing?

4. Why does intellectualizing keep us from growing spiritually?

    _____

5. How will an intellectual treat the Bible, and where will this lead him?

    _____

6. How will an intellectual person misuse reasoning?

    _____

7. How should we learn to reason?

    _____

8. How should every Christian treat change?

    _____

CHAPTER 7

John 14:26, John 16:13-14; Matthew 7:24-25

Some of the synonyms for *spiritualize* in the thesaurus are actually the same as for the word *spiritual*. They are "devout, Godly, immaterial, intangible, religious, supernatural and unearthly." The dictionary defines spiritualize as "to make spiritual; deprive of materiality or worldliness. To give a spiritual sense or meaning to."

As I said in the previous chapter, if we intellectualize God's Word, we silence His voice toward us. If we depend on our own mind by mentally striving rather than depending on the leading of the Holy Spirit, we silence His ministry to us. Because of the mental barrier of intellectualizing, we leave God with very limited avenues to reach us. He tries to speak to us, but we rarely hear Him. We know He exists, so we begin to look to the only means we have left to try to understand His character and His will for our lives; we turn to our circumstances and try to see the hand of God in them.

In the church, people are constantly trying to figure out what God is saying to them through their circumstances. They are spiritualizing both their successes and their failures and are constantly trying to read into every trivial occurrence for His guidance and direction. The will of God is a very unstable thing to a person who spiritualizes and uses their circumstances to judge either God's favor or His disapproval toward them. They are doing exactly what the heathen or pagans do. A storm that kills some in the village is read as a sign that the god of weather is angry with them. In this same way, one time a Christian thinks God is for their project, the next time they think He is against it. Or they conclude that He must be trying to teach them something. Then they rack their brains trying to figure out what it is He is trying to teach them. Sometimes they even come up with the reason for every unanswered prayer. They say that God answered, but He answered with a "no." Because of being so self-centered, these people have a whole justification or alibi system set up for God because He answered them with a "no." Since they are unsure of the will of God, they justify their every move and God gets wrongfully blamed.

There is also a question as to our integrity and stewardship when we are spending all our time mentally striving to solve our problems or situations. We are functioning in our everyday duties but not with wholeheartedness or focus. The mind trap of spiritualizing will assign spiritual dimensions to the natural occurrences in our lives leading to mental confusion.

When we discussed staying in the rest of God, we saw that He sent us the Holy Spirit to meet our every need.

In John 14:26 we read:

> *"But the Comforter, which is the Holy Ghost, whom the Father will send in my name, he shall teach you all things, and bring all things to your remembrance, whatsoever I have said unto you."*

In John 16:13–14 we read:

> *"Howbeit when he, the Spirit of truth, is come, he will guide you into all truth: for he shall not speak of himself; but whatsoever he shall hear, that shall he speak: and he will show you things to come."*

These Scriptures show us how important placing our trust in the Holy Spirit is to staying in the rest of our soul. We must focus ourselves on these two Scriptures and ask the Holy Spirit to reveal hidden knowledge to us in our everyday life, so we can see the truth in every situation we are facing. If we have made Jesus the Lord of our lives, then He should be the master of everything that concerns us. This means we take Him at His Word above everyone else and above everything else.

In Romans 10:9–13 God says:

> *"If thou shalt confess with thy mouth the Lord Jesus, and shalt believe in thine heart that God hath raised him from the dead, thou shalt be saved. For with the heart man believeth unto righteousness; and with the mouth confession is made unto salvation. For the Scripture saith, whosoever believeth on him shall not be ashamed. For there is no difference between the Jew and the Greek: for the same Lord over all is rich unto all that call upon him. For whosoever shall call upon the name of the Lord shall be saved."*

Note here that man believes to righteousness, not self-righteousness. Self-righteousness is when we do things in our own strength. We are not to function in our own strength when it comes to getting answers to prayer, growing ourselves up, or comparing our spiritual growth to that of others. We are not to be striving in the flesh with anything pertaining to life and godliness. The salvation we have been given includes not only eternal life, but also being healed, delivered, and made whole. If we believe in our hearts what God says to us in His Word and if we confess the Word out of our mouth to Him, it will bring us salvation in every situation.

A person who has a habit of spiritualizing and who is stuck in this mind trap always has a fifty-fifty chance that either the devil or God will direct their circumstances. An example of spiritualizing I recall is of a woman who was married to a man from another country. Every so often, he needed his green card renewed. They prayed for God's will before going to renew the card, but while they were standing in line, the window closed. They happened to be in line at closing time, and because of this they concluded, "I guess God doesn't want us to get the green card renewed." Why blame God for the office closing? If they prayed and received God's will to have the green card renewed, then this is what will happen and the office closing doesn't change what was received in prayer. Also, why spiritualize that it was His will to close the window before their card was stamped. Sometimes we have to be persistent. We can't forget what we prayed, received, and dismiss our faith in what we already have, so to speak, our green card stamped. What has been received in prayer from the spiritual world has a time delay until it manifests itself in the natural world. Getting their green card renewed is what was received in prayer—this is the key that should keep them focused and their faith working for them.

In this case, the couple was married and they had children. It was important for their family to stay together in this country. God is very practical, and we need to be too. The office closing was an annoying hindrance, but they did not have to spiritualize that as meaning God did not want the card to be renewed. Sometimes as Christians, we are looking for the hand of God in every circumstance of our lives and we go to extremes to try to figure out God's will, when ordinary common sense is the best point of view. If our mind is focused on the Word, we can hold onto what we have received in prayer and walk it through knowing we already have the result.

Matthew 7:24–27 is a good example of this:

> *"Therefore, whosoever heareth these sayings of mine, and doeth them, I will liken him unto a wise man, which built his house upon a rock: And the rain descended, and the floods came, and the winds blew, and beat upon that house; and it fell not: for it was founded upon a rock. And everyone that heareth these sayings of mine, and doeth them not, shall be likened unto a foolish man, which built his house upon the sand: And the rain descended, and the*

*floods came, and the winds blew, and beat upon
that house; and it fell: and great was the fall of it."*

The word *rock* in this story refers to the Word. If our house or life is built on the Word of God, it will stand the storms of life. If we build our foundation on the Word, we will not be tossed about when the storms come. We can know the end result and hold our minds at rest until our circumstances reflect what we received. This is being doers of the Word not just hearers only. We need to move beyond just believing only to also receiving from God. When a person believes only, he has the complete weight of the problem on himself. We need to both believe and receive from God.

The familiar question is, "Do I have enough faith?" This is not the place God wants us to be. We are to keep His words in our heart as our basis for trust. Because of His trustworthiness, we can believe His words, which are the basis for our faith. With this foundation, we will speak faith-filled words. They will resist any conflicting circumstances, unbelief in our minds, or any other statements from people, until the answer arrives. Receiving His promises and continually speaking the end result is not hard work and keeps our focus on God, not on us. We have to know that our petitions are already accomplished in the spirit realm, and they have an appointed time in the natural realm.

We need to remember to ask ourselves, "Who am I?" If our identity is based on how many degrees we have after our name or based on all our accomplishments in this life, then we have forgotten who God says we are.

In Ephesians 2:8–10 it says:

*"For by grace are ye saved through faith; and that
not of yourselves: it is the gift of God: Not of works,
lest any man should boast. For we are his workmanship, created in Christ Jesus unto good works, which
God hath before ordained that we should walk in
them."*

This is our real identity. We are made by Him. We are His workmanship. We are His masterpiece. Second Corinthians 5:17 says we are a new creature made by God. We are not to be in works of our own doing. Our hands should be doing the good works of God. When works are created by the Holy Spirit, everyone increases and it happens without mental striving. This means all our plans have to be put before God in prayer. His will has to be received, and it will be done by the Holy Spirit. Our trust has to be in God for everything; this way our minds can remain stable in the rest and not waver while we walk through the circumstances of our lives.

Spiritualizing is the basis of most primitive religions. The Bible tells us that pagan gods are deaf and dumb and their images are made of wood, clay, or stone. How then can they hear requests and answer them? The people who make them with their hands assign to them their own characteristics and abilities. They give the idols power over themselves and live in fear of them. If it stops raining for several months, they believe the gods must be angry. If it rains so much it floods, they believe the gods are angry again. If the weather is good, they think the gods are pleased. This is the way primitive people second guess the pleasure or displeasure of their gods with them. Should we be spiritualizing like pagans?

Job said in chapter 1:21: *"Naked came I out of my mother's womb, and naked shall I return thither: the Lord gave, and the Lord hath taken away; blessed be the name of the Lord."*

Job made this statement after losing his children and all his earthly possessions. Job's protective hedge was down because of his fear. Job made seventy-four different false accusations against God. He was offended, rejected, and depressed over what he thought God had taken from him or done to him. When we do not have our enemy identified, we have to spiritualize. The words Job said actually exposed his lack of knowledge of God's character, and he became the devil's advocate. John 10:10 says, *"The thief cometh not, but for to steal, and to kill, and to destroy: I am come that they might have life, and that they might have it more abundantly."* If stealing, killing, and destroying are in our lives or affecting our family in some way, it is not coming from the hand of God. God is not the source of our losses. I often see it this way in my life. The devil desires to steal me from the Word, kill my vision, and destroy my hope, but I submit myself to God and resist the devil, and he flees from me. Submitting to God means I take Him at His Word and I do not forget what I have received from Him. Job eventually changed his thinking toward God and received abundantly from God in the end. He says in Job 6:23–25: *"Teach me, and I will hold my tongue: and cause me to understand wherein I have erred. How forcible are right words!"*

Job is now considering that his words may have been part of his problem. In Job 42:3–6, we see what happens when he finally turns to God: *"Therefore have I uttered that I understood not; things too wonderful for me, which I knew not. Wherefore I abhor myself, and repent in dust and ashes."*

After Job realized his mistake of attributing his illness, losses, and calamities to God, he repented. Job got past his spiritualizing and identified his true enemy. He recognized that God was not his enemy and He did not cause his losses. From that point on, Job experienced a renewed relationship with God and He delivered Job. In the end, the Lord also gave him twice as much as he had before.

Many Christians in the church today are using the statements of Job as their justification for unanswered prayer. They reason that their calamities, losses, and personal tragedies are caused by God. They think the reason they are where they are is because it is God's plan for their lives. Many others believe their suffering is God's hand in their lives to make them increase in patience or for some other character training. They also justify why they are staying as babes instead of growing up and maturing.

I was told of a little girl whose mother died and her uncle explained to her, "God took your mother because He wanted her to be with Him." At his statement, the child became confused and divided in her spirit. On the one hand, she wanted to believe God was a good God, but yet she felt He robbed her of her mother's love and care. Since her mother died, she has tried to love God like she did before but now she has a hard time trusting Him. She keeps wondering what He will take away from her next. We can see how dangerous spiritualizing can be. The well-meaning words of her uncle to try to comfort her confused her instead.

Another example is one of a faithful woman who served in her church for many years. She was tired and her right knee hurt, but she could not bring herself to step down and give her job to someone else. Instead, she said, "God put my knee out, so I would slow down." Can we see how *self* is elevated and the character of God is perverted? The God who promises life abundant is not in the business of putting out knees!

When a person has a habit of spiritualizing, it leads to repeated times of offense and rejection. We can usually find legalism and a religious spirit dominating these people's lives. Legalism is the heavy hand of the law without the application of the Spirit. A religious spirit is a hard taskmaster to serve because the person is usually not appropriating blessings in faith but operating out of fear. There is a tremendous amount of obligation and pressure to be *right*, and that is when the yoke becomes too heavy to bear.

Many people have the concept that once they decide to live by the Word of God, the enemy is going to leave them alone. This is not true, but a simple misconception. Instead, the devil will try to thwart their decision to become a believer. He will come at them with everything he can think, and it will take real decisiveness and trust in God to continue in the Word. Jesus said in Hebrews 13:5b says, "I will never leave you, nor forsake you." We have the Holy Spirit as our guide into all truth. He is our teacher. One of the Scriptures the Holy Spirit revealed to Dennis and me still helps us whenever a decision needs to be made. It is found in Matthew 7:7–8:

> *"Ask, and it shall be given you; seek, and ye shall find; knock, and it shall be opened unto you: For everyone that asketh receiveth; and he the seeketh findeth; and to him that knocketh it shall be opened."*

Another one we use frequently is found in Revelation 3:8:

> *"I know thy works: behold, I have set before thee an open door, and no man can shut it: for thou hast a little strength, and hast kept my word, and hast not denied my name."*

We ask and receive God's wisdom and His will for a different job, a new home, or maybe a vacation when there are multiple choices. We then seek and find, believing we will find the wisdom. This means our part is to seek every means of information that is available to us. In seeking, we are to tap into a variety of sources including various interviews with people, checking the real estate market, and all kinds of travel brochures. Talking to people can be a great resource. We can also be led in our hearts. God promises us that we will find wisdom, and He will help us make the right decision. In Proverbs, wisdom is referred to as a female allegorical figure. Everyone can have access to the wisdom of God, and His wisdom always takes us down a peaceful path. We will hear the wisdom in the words, and it will confirm the knowledge of His direction we already have in our heart. The seeking will lead to finding the most peaceful blessing. When we have reached this place, we will knock and the door will be opened to us.

Revelation 3:8 says, *"It is a door no man can close."* This verse can be a great comfort to the person who fears making the wrong decision. When seeking and finding information, we will know that the door God has opened for us, no one can close. By faith we will find it and make the right decision. If we cannot close the door and neither can any other person involved in the decision close the door, we will know it is the will of God and we can step through with confidence and peace in our hearts.

This is using natural elements to secure the will of God, but it is not justifying our actions by stating it must be God's will. When we prayed for wisdom and His will, we already knew there was a new job, home, or vacation on the horizon. It was the means to bring it to us where the wisdom, seeking, and finding came in.

It is important to note these Scriptures were a personal revelation to us. They were said to our hearts while watching a Christian preacher on TV. We know the Scripture in Revelation 3:8 is stating the attributes of the first-century church in Philadelphia; however, the verse also spoke to our own personal attributes of having little strength compared to Jesus. We have kept His Word and not denied His Name. The Holy Spirit spoke these Scriptures and their applications to our lives. If others take these Scriptures and say they will work for them without consulting the Holy Spirit and receiving His revelation for their lives, they will become a presumption. We have always used this statement as a rule, "Your revelation becomes my presumption." We cannot copy each other's revelations. The Holy Spirit gives us our own tailor-made revelation. Those are the only ones that really work.

1. What problem is caused by a believer who looks for God in their circumstances?

    _____

2. What realm will we find the works of God?

    _____

3. What is the result of a believer who tries to spiritualize their position of defeat?

    _____

4. What benefit do we lose when we let the circumstances guide our direction?

    _____

5. Spiritualizing can take the place of "whom" in trying to find out the will of God?

    _____

6. What will the Word of God do for us when we are seeking the will of God for direction?

    _____

7. Where does faith begin in the life of the believer?

    _____

8. What Scripture is the dividing line of cause and effect in a believer's life?

    _____

9. What can a believer learn from the lesson Job experienced?

    _____

10. Remember, one man's revelation is another man's presumption.

    _____

CHAPTER 8

Pride

1 Corinthians 13:4–8; Psalm 10:4

The synonyms for *pride* in the thesaurus are "arrogance, conceit, self-importance, vainglory, boastfulness, haughtiness, and narcissism." Narcissism is excessive self-admiration or self-love. A prideful person is one who is overly self-centered, only thinks of themselves and everything they do is regarding *self.* The dictionary says of *pride* "an overly high opinion of oneself; exaggerated self-esteem, conceit, haughty behavior resulting from pride and arrogance."

There are scriptural examples of pride in Numbers 24:1–9. These passages are on the right thinking or positive side of pride concerning Balak, the king of Moab. Balak was afraid of the sudden appearance of the people of Israel who came out of the land of Egypt. He sent for Balaam to curse these people. When Balaam saw that it pleased the Lord to bless Israel, he could not curse them, but instead he blessed them.

In Number 24:9 we read, *"Blessed is everyone who blesses you and cursed is everyone who curses you."* Who is Balaam talking about? He is talking about Israel. This is what Balaam prophesied as he saw the great multitude camped tribe by tribe with their tents. In God's eyes, Israel was exalted as His covenant people and God took pride in them and protected them from the King of Moab. This was rightful pride on God's part.

In Samuel 22:33 David says, *"God is my strong fortress; and He sets the blameless in His way."* This is David's Psalm of Deliverance. It is his testimony. David knows that his strength comes from the Lord, his rock. David is proud of the Lord. This is an example of rightful pride. In verse 47 David continues to exalt God: "*The Lord liveth; and blessed be my rock; and exalted be the God of the rock of my salvation."*

Joshua 4:14 is another example of right-thinking with pride or rightful pride. It says in the King James, *"On that day the Lord magnified Joshua in the sight of all Israel and they feared him as they feared Moses all the days of his life."* After Moses died, Joshua became their new leader and prepared the people to cross over the Jordan River. The Lord God made Joshua important in the people's sight so they would be proud of him and accept him as their new leader.

This is the positive side of pride that makes it right to be exalted and revered. We do this to some extent to our pastors. We exalt and revere them. That is where the title *Reverend* came from. Our ministers are "revered ones." Our safety as believers depends on their integrity. We need to have a man of integrity over us, someone we can look to for guidance and protection. They can give us spiritual insight, direction as he prays for us and counsels us. We can share in his blessings and the anointing that is on him. It can come on us as well, as our portion.

In 2 Samuel 5:12 it says, *"And David perceived that the Lord had established him king over Israel and had exalted his kingdom for His people Israel's sake."* There will be times when God will exalt men and put them in high positions when it is for the benefit of the people. And that is why we need to pray for God's people to be in places of leadership in our country.

In 1 Chronicles 29:25 David's son Solomon is exalted: "*The Lord highly exalted Solomon in the sight of all Israel and bestowed on him royal splendor such as no king over Israel ever had before."*

When Solomon took over David's throne, the Lord exalted him to such a level that King Solomon's splendor was the talk of the ancient world. The Lord was so proud of King Solomon and His people that He wanted his reputation to go far and wide throughout all the ancient lands to all the people.

Adonijah, David's son, plotted to seize the kingdom and take the throne from his brother Solomon, the rightful heir to the throne. He exalted himself, saying, *"I will be king."* Adonijah is an example of wrongful pride. His plans were contrary to God's sovereign plans. He prepared for himself chariots and horsemen with fifty men to run before him, and he tried to seize the kingdom for himself. King David was well advanced in years by this time, and while Adonijah and his brothers feasted, David's wife, Bathsheba went to him and asked if he had definitely said Solomon would sit on the throne after him. She also informed him that Adonijah was setting up his throne and all the people were looking to him to be the next king. David not only appointed Solomon king but had the priest anoint him with oil. Then they blew the trumpet, and all the people said, "Long live King Solomon!" Adonijah eventually submitted to Solomon's rule. The entire story of Adonijah's prideful self-exaltation is found in 1 Kings, chapter 1.

In 2 Chronicles 32:26 it says that King Hezekiah had a high heart. He was proud but smart enough to *"humble himself for the pride of his heart, both he and the inhabitants of Jerusalem, so that the wrath of the Lord came not upon them in the days of Hezekiah."* Hezekiah knew that the Lord hated wrongful pride and was careful to protect himself and the inhabitants of Jerusalem by humbling himself.

When we talk, we know within ourselves which one we are indulging in—rightful or wrongful pride. It all depends on who gets the glory! If it is wrongful pride, we will strive to get the glory, and if it is rightful pride, we will let God have the glory.

In Job 33:17 it says that God's purpose for dreams is *"that he may withdraw man from his purpose, and hide pride from man."* It is very easy for us to plan our day and go off in our own strength without even considering God's plans for our lives, or we can get into such a routine or rut that we cannot even hear God's voice. That is why in Job it says God brings dreams in the night seasons to stop man from achieving his prideful purposes and those plans that may be injurious to him. God is always concerned for our welfare and well-being.

Psalm 10:4 reads, *"The wicked, through the pride of his countenance, will not seek after God: God is not in all his thoughts."* The prideful person does not have God as their source but relies upon himself. God is not in the thoughts of the wicked and prideful person because he is too self-centered to consider God. The selfish, prideful person prefers to give the credit to himself. When he boasts, he boasts of all his accomplishments and that he is a self-made man. He does not realize there is a cost to serve the master of pride.

Psalm 12:3 says, *"The Lord shall cut off all flattering lips, and the tongue that speaks proud things."* This may sound severe but God hates self-exaltation and flattering lips. Calculated praise of others for gain is an abomination to Him. He wants us to have pure motives and speak from truthful hearts.

I have put together a list of the costs of pride found in the Scriptures:

1. The prideful person will not seek God (Psalm 10:4).

2. A prideful person slanders his neighbor; he will be cut off (Psalm 101:5).

3. The Lord hates a proud look (Proverbs 6:17).

4. Shame comes with pride (Proverbs 11:2).

5. Pride brings contention (Proverbs 13:10).

6. The mouth of the foolish has a rod of pride (Proverbs 14:3).

7. The house of the proud will be destroyed (Proverbs 15:25).

8.   The proud in heart is an abomination to the Lord (Proverbs 16:5).

9.   Pride goes before destruction, a haughty spirit before a fall (Proverbs 16:18).

10. A proud heart is sin (Proverbs 21:4).

11. A proud heart stirs up strife (Proverbs 28:25).

12. A man's pride shall bring him low (Proverbs 29:23).

13. The lofty looks of man shall be humbled (Isaiah 2:11-12, 17).

14. God resists the proud (James 4:6, 1 Peter 5:5).

Pride is the springboard that leads us into sin and error. Pride is the vehicle that gets us into a lot of trouble. Jesus gave us only one law to live by under the new covenant, the law of love. Pride is the opposite of love.

First Corinthians 13 tells us the attributes of love. Verse 4 and 5 says, *"Love flaunts not itself, is not puffed up, does not behave itself unseemly, seeks not her own."* The reverse of these statements is a good description of pride. Pride flaunts itself, is puffed up, behaves itself unseemly; and pride definitely seeks her own! If we look at any sin or trouble we have gotten ourselves into, we can usually find that the element of pride was involved. Jesus said if we follow the law of love, we will keep all the other commandments. However, if we follow after pride, we will break them all.

Pride was Satan's downfall and has taken him into every conceivable perversion of God's ways ever since. Satan was the worship leader in heaven. He had great gifts and was a beautiful heavenly being. Yet he was so proud of himself that he rebelled and wanted to be exalted higher than God. Pride is a deadly trap. It cuts us off from the truth. When we fall into pride, we become unteachable like the scribes and the Pharisees who thought they knew it all and so missed their own salvation.

Pride also sets us up for humiliation. Matthew 23:12 says, *"And whosoever shall exalt himself shall be abased."* It is much better to be humble than to be humiliated. Jesus gives us an illustration of this in Luke 14:8–9 in *the Amplified Bible*:

> *"When you are invited by anyone to a marriage feast, do not recline on the chief seat, in the place of honor, lest a more distinguished person than you has been invited by him; And he who invited both of you will come to you and say, Let this man have the place you have taken. Then with humiliation and a guilty sense of impropriety you will begin to take the lowest place."*

We can observe some pride with sibling rivalry next. Miriam, Moses's sister, got into wrongful pride and made the mistake of exalting herself in the twelfth chapter of Numbers. She and Aaron, Moses's brother, spoke against Moses in verse 2. They said, *"Has the Lord only spoken by Moses? Has he not also spoken by us?"* In other words, they took pride in themselves over him and asked, "What's so great about Moses? We are just as spiritual and Godly as he is!" They challenged God for choosing Moses to lead the children of Israel out of Egypt instead of them. Scripture says the Lord heard it and called Moses, Aaron, and Miriam together. He told them that He spoke to His prophets and prophetesses in dreams and visions, but to Moses he had spoken face-to-face. How could Aaron and Miriam compare themselves to Moses? After this rebuke, the Lord departed, and as the cloud vanished, they saw that Miriam was covered with leprosy.

Immediately, Moses cried out to the Lord to heal her. God said in Numbers 12:14: *"If her father had but spit in her face, should she not be ashamed seven days? Let her be shut out from the camp for seven days, and after that let her be received in again."*

Miriam, a prophetess, was humiliated in front of all the people of Israel because she exalted herself. She did it because of self-pride.

Yet God heard Moses's compassionate prayer for her and after seven days removed her leprosy so she could join her people again within the camp.

It is interesting that leprosy is the disease that Miriam contracted as a result of pride. When someone has leprosy, the nerve fibers become anesthetized, which leads to muscle paralysis. Because of the paralysis, the extremities are not used and because of decreased circulation, they become atrophied or shriveled up. The leprous person loses the use of their extremities due to this insufficient blood flow.

Lepers are also prone to sustaining injuries that go undetected because of the numbness in their members. There have been actual cases where rodents ate the fingers, toes, and even noses of lepers while they slept and they were unaware of it due to a lack of feeling in these parts!

Pride can be a spiritual leprosy in the body of Christ. First, numbness to the truth sets in. The prideful person has an "I already know it all!" mentality so that anything they hear that is different from their own thinking is rejected. If they hear anything different from what they believe, they think it must be an error. This *numb* mindset or anesthesia leads to spiritual paralysis. Many Christians stay spiritual infants all their lives. They stop moving forward and growing because they stop listening and learning. This mind-set hinders the flow of life-giving blood from God. They cease to be adequately nourished and are unable to give nourishment to others. The enemy, like a rodent, continues to gnaw at them and deceive them as they lie in a numb stupor.

All of us continue to see areas of pride in our lives. One that we may not have noticed is called the pride of knowledge. When we grow in the knowledge of the Lord, we may want others to believe the same as we believe or we may want the pastor of our church to teach exactly as we would teach. We say to ourselves, "The pastor doesn't have the knowledge I have in this area, so he really doesn't know what he's talking about!" But when we become proud of our own knowledge in an area, we fall into wrongful pride. We fall into the mind trap of pride. If we spread these thoughts in the church, we exalt ourselves in our own eyes and at the same time bring division into the church and undermine the ministry.

On the other hand, if we place our faith in God to speak through the pastor or other teachers, then we will receive something from God through them. We cannot stifle others in their individual growth, and we cannot elevate ourselves at the cost of those around us.

The *love* chapter in 1 Corinthians 13:4–8 explains to us the characteristics that God wants us to exhibit in our lives. These are the qualities we all need to have established in our souls. They have already been shed abroad in our hearts. Every time I read through these passages, I wonder how I can possibly become a person like this. Yet Romans 5:5 tells us: *"And hope maketh not ashamed; because the love of God is shed abroad in our hearts by the Holy Ghost which is given unto us."*

The *love of God* has already been poured into our hearts through the work of our Lord Jesus on the cross. God's characteristics of love have already been given to us by the Holy Spirit. When we are living in the strength of the love that is in our spirit-man, these qualities can easily flow out to those around us.

One of these characteristics is that we do not seek our own. Remember, we are all co-laborers with God. We are to be willing to listen, learn, and grow. When God energizes some knowledge we have been given, it will produce fruit when shared at the appropriate time. It is God who is at work within us to *"will and to do of His good pleasure"* (Philippians 2:13).

Another characteristic of love is that it does not take into account a suffered wrong. Our natural man makes very detailed accounts of every wrong it has ever suffered from anyone, and the *memory of an elephant* usually goes along with that list! We carry these grievances around like baggage in our minds and *recall* brings back things that happened to us or things people said to us years ago. These memories come back to haunt and torment us. God wants us to be free from all this excess baggage, and He has given us the way through the act of forgiveness and laying every care on Him.

1. How do you know if you are in a place of wrongful pride?

   _____

2. Who is the source of prideful thinking?

   _____

3. What characteristic of God is opposite of pride?

   _____

4. When does praise of others become a problem for the believer?

   _____

5. Describe some of the attributes of pride.

   _____

6. What does it mean to be not teachable?

   _____

7. Why is the pride of knowledge a bad trait?

   _____

8. What is the fruit of the pride of knowledge?

   _____

CHAPTER 9

Jeremiah 1:12; Proverbs 29:20, Proverbs 21:5

Some of the synonyms for the word *impulsiveness* in the thesaurus are "impetuosity, indiscretion, rashness and hastiness." Impulsive actions are done in haste, out of rashness and the person does not think before acting or reacting. The dictionary definition of impulsiveness is "an incitement to action arising from a state of mind or some external stimulus. A sudden inclination to act without conscious thought."

Impulsiveness is not always negative. On the right-thinking side, we have an example of Abigail's constructive impulsiveness in 1 Samuel 25. She brought food to David and his mighty men, and she saved her husband Nabal's life by her positive, impulsive act. Here is a picture of good haste when necessary, and her act was calculated to help the situation.

In the first part of this chapter, we learn Samuel the prophet has died. David and his men were camped on Nabal's land and were protecting it, but they were hungry and needed food. Because they had been protecting his land, they felt Nabal owed them his gratitude. So David sent messengers to Nabal, Abigail's husband, because he had great possessions and thousands of sheep. But when David's messengers asked Nabal for food, he gave them a nasty reply in verse 10:

*And Nabal answered David's servants, and said,
"Who is David? And who is the son of Jesse? There
be many servants now a days that break away every
man from his master. Shall I then take my bread,
and my water, and my flesh that I have killed for my
shearers, and give it unto men, whom I know not
whence they be?"*

David's servants went back and told David everything Nabal said. At this, David became fighting mad and said to his men, *"Gird ye on every man his sword." And they girded on every man his sword; and David also girded on his sword: and there went up after David about four hundred men; and two hundred abode by the stuff* (1 Samuel 25:13) David told his men to arm themselves. They planned to kill Nabal and all the men of his household for his reply to them, but a young man told Abigail what Nabal said to David's messengers. We read of her positive impulsiveness in verse 18:

*"Then Abigail made haste, and took two hundred
loaves, and two bottles of wine, and five sheep ready
dressed, and five measures of parched corn, and a
hundred clusters of raisins, and two hundred cakes
of figs, and laid them on asses."*

Abigail told her servants to go on before her and that she would come after them, but she did not tell her husband, Nabal, what she was doing. She rode on a donkey, and when she came down the hillside, David and his men met her caravan of food. When she saw David, she quickly got off her animal, fell at his feet, and said:

*Upon me, my lord, upon me let this iniquity be:
and let thine handmaid, I pray thee, speak in thine
audience, and hear the words of thine handmaid.
Let not my Lord, I pray thee regard this man of*

Belial, even Nabal for as his name is, so is he. Nabal is his name and folly is with him.

Nabal means "son of worthlessness, wickedness, evil . . . it is a Kurdish term." Abigail goes on to implore David:

> *But I, thine handmaid saw not the young men of my lord, whom thou didst send. Now therefore, my lord, As the Lord liveth and as thy soul liveth, seeing the Lord hath withholden thee from coming to shed blood and from avenging thyself with thine own hand...*

Abigail begged David to forgive Nabal's foolishness. She even took the blame for him by saying she did not see his men. She advised David and calmed him down from his rage to get even for Nabal's affront to him and his men. Abigail told David that taking out his revenge on Nabal was below him because God had such good and high plans for his life to appoint him ruler over Israel. She told him that if he wiped out Nabal and every male in his household now, it would be a grief and offense to him later in his heart. She urged him not to avenge himself. To her plea, David replied:

> *"Blessed be the Lord God of Israel, who sent you this day to meet me: And blessed be thy advice, and blessed be you, who has kept me this day from coming to shed blood, and from avenging myself with my own hand. For in every deed, and the Lord God of Israel liveth, who has kept me back from hurting you, except thou had hasted and came to meet me, surely there had not been left unto Nabal by the morning light . . ."*

David received the food that she brought him and blessed her, saying, *"Go up in peace to thine house; see, I have hearkened to thy voice, and have accepted thy person."*

Because she hurried to meet David, she prevented the calamity and bloodshed on her husband and his entire household. Here is a picture of a proper hurrying—when it is of God and when it is positive impulsiveness. There are times when we have to drop everything and do what God tells us to do. When He says, "go," we go! We have to drop everything and do it!

We have another example of positive impulsiveness in the instructions given for the end time event in Matthew 24:16–22. It says when the abomination of desolation is set up in the Temple, those who are in Judea are to flee to the mountains. They are not to come down from the rooftops or take anything out of their houses. Scripture says it will be more difficult for mothers with babies and small children to flee fast, but they are to be ready to go. This is the rightful hastening that we are to have within us when God tells us to leave. We have to be ready to move, but when God says to move, there is no pressure put on the person. One way to recognize the source is that when the word comes from God, it is without pressure.

The Passover is another example of positive impulsiveness. God told Israel they would have to be ready to move quickly when He gave the word to leave Egypt. He prepared them ahead of time. He told them exactly what to do. They were to take a few things and keep their houses in order. Every detail was foretold to them by God, even the instructions to use unleavened bread because it did not take a long time to rise. When it is a leading from God, it is without pressure and He will give you the instructions and strength to do it. The children of Israel were prepared to leave whenever God gave them the word.

In Jeremiah 1:12 we read, *"Then said the Lord unto me, 'Thou hast well seen: for I will hasten my word to perform it.'"* God does speed up His Word at times. He hastens His Word to perform it. This is an encouraging passage. It shows that there are times of speedy fulfillment for situations.

On the wrong-thinking side of impulsiveness, we can fall for this trap and we do not think ahead, but we just react. Doctor Devil taps our knee and up jerks our foot in reaction to the tap! Many times this type of reaction is aggravated by the words of our mouths.

Hasty words are a product of impulsiveness. Words spoken in the heat of the moment can be regretted for years to come.

Proverbs 29:20 says, *"See thou a man that is hasty in his words, there is more hope of a fool than of him."* Sometimes it can cost us a friendship, a job, or a reputation. When we remember them, we need to repent of them. The impulsive person seems to have a constant need for change, jumping from one half-finished project to another. Their lives are characterized by big plans made of *half-baked* ideas with shaky foundations. These are all symptoms of impulsiveness.

Years ago, some friends of ours decided to invest in a somewhat risky business deal after they heard a sales pitch that promised them fantastic returns. "Maybe we should check with our financial advisor about this first," suggested the wife. "No," answered her husband, "he'll tell us not to do it." That is impulsiveness talking! After learning a hard lesson, this couple shared with us their new policy: "If it can't wait twenty-four hours while we pray and seek advice, we don't do it, buy it, or sell it!"

We have all heard story after story of people with the best intentions running out in front of God because of what they thought was His word for them. Or perhaps they did receive a word from God, but they never stopped to ask Him for further instructions. One young couple received a prophecy telling them that they were to go to Africa as missionaries. They were so excited that they immediately began selling everything they had. Three years later, the door to Africa opened. In the meantime, they had no furniture to sit on! They had never prayed and asked God when.

In 1 Chronicles 13:1–4 we see David's impulsiveness:

> *"And David said unto all the congregation of Israel, 'If it seem good unto you, and that it be the Lord our God, let us send abroad unto our brethren everywhere, that are left in all the land of Israel, and with them also the priests and the Levites which are in their cities and their suburbs, that they may gather themselves unto us: And let us bring again the ark of our God to us: for we enquired not at it*

*in the days of Saul.' And all the congregation said
that they would do so: for the thing was right in the
eyes of all the people."*

David made sure it was God's will that the ark be returned to the congregation of Israel. He got plenty of counsel, and everyone was in agreement with him that the ark should be returned. At first consideration, this does not look like an impulsive act. So where did David go wrong? As we read on, we find the children of Israel gathered together, singing, dancing, and parading. Two men, Uzza and Ahio, drove the cart on which the ark was placed. When one of the oxen suddenly stumbled, Uzza, in a well-intentioned act of impulsiveness, reached out and grabbed the ark to keep it from falling to the ground. Verse 10 says: *"And the anger of the Lord was kindled against Uzza, and he smote him, because he put his hand to the ark: and there he died before God."*

God had told the people that no one was to touch the ark except the priests. Uzza's sudden death put a damper on their parade and festivities, and the project of moving the ark was aborted. Later in chapter 15, David takes the ark project up again after evidently asking more questions of God. In verses 12 and 13, he explains where he made his error:

*"And said unto them, Ye are the chief of the fathers
of the Levites: sanctify yourselves, both ye and your
brethren, that ye may bring up the ark of the Lord
God of Israel unto the place that I have prepared for
it. For because you did it not at the first, the Lord
your God made a breach upon us, for that he sought
Him not after the due order."*

David never stopped to ask God how He wanted the task accomplished, and it cost one man his life. We need to take all our plans to God and wait with patience for His instructions. If our plans are sound and God confirms them in our hearts, we need to seek

Him for how and when to proceed. If we forget to do this, we may be responsible for the death of a well-intentioned plan.

Proverbs 21:5 says, *"The thoughts of the diligent tend only to plenteousness, but to every one that is hasty, only to want."* A reactor does not think before jumping into things. A reactor is not acting as a co-laborer with God. What if we know we are a reactor? When we realize that we have a problem with impulsiveness and that we are a reactor, we are already 50 percent out of it! Just knowing it is half the battle. A reactor is in the driver's seat and has left God and all their passengers behind.

It is not Godly to act as a reactor. We are to respond to things, not react. If we put our foot in our mouth most of the time or we react in acts that have pressure on them, we are walking in impulsiveness. If we do not think through our actions before we do them, we are walking in impulsiveness. If we know we are a reactor and we keep getting caught in these situations, it is time to say, "We need to get a hold of ourselves now!" Remember, if an idea to do something has pressure on it, it is from the devil. God's leading results in peace of mind.

Our emotions have to be controlled if our soul is to be established in God. When our soul is established, our emotions will be controlled. We cannot have one without the other. All it takes is an act of our will. It does not mean that reacting and impulsiveness in our lives is going to stop immediately, but once we start seeing it, we can eventually overcome it.

A man called me on the telephone and said, "I have no control over my emotions, none whatsoever!" I said to him, "I'm glad you said that because now you're halfway out! Now it's just a matter of practicing." That is all it takes, just practice! And we are probably going to practice because when we get caught in the mind trap of impulsiveness, it is not a very pleasant experience!

Every time it happens, we are going to know it, because the Holy Spirit will impress our spirit. We can say to ourselves, "There I go again. I jumped ahead too fast. I should have talked to You first. I reacted again. Father, I repent, in the Name of Jesus. I thank You, Holy Spirit, that I have a covenant with You. You are showing me my reactions. You are showing me a way out of this. You are showing me how not to do it again. You are giving me an alternate way of responding."

As in David's case, his not inquiring of the Lord as to how to bring back the ark resulted in a man's death. Our impulsiveness could have its own consequences or costs as well. I cannot say to you, "This is what works for me. You can do it too." No. I am not your best advisor. The Holy Spirit within us will show us how to respond because he knows us from the inside out. I only know you from the outside in!

1. Whose direction are we taking when we react in impulsiveness?

_____

2. Can an impulsive action be good?

_____

3. What are the differences between reacting versus responding?

_____

4. How should we learn to respond?

_____

5. What kind of a trail does the impulsive person leave?

_____

6. What if we know we are a reactor?

_____

7. What kind of a person does not think about their actions?

    _____

8. What kind of a leading is it when it has pressure attached to it?

    _____

Affliction

Mark 4:14–20; 2 Corinthians
12:7–10; James 1:2–4

Some of the synonyms in the thesaurus for *affliction* are "beset, grieve, plague, torment, encompass, surround, encircle, harass, provoke, smite, and distress."

In the dictionary, *affliction* implies pain, suffering, or distress imposed by illness, loss, or misfortune. It means "to strike down, to cause pain or suffering, to distress very much, to overthrow, to injure, to cause pressure, stress, and tension."

All the other mind traps have a positive or right-thinking side to them except assumption and affliction. There is nothing positive about pressures that come in this life to annihilate us. In Mark 4:14–20 we see that after the Word has been sown in our heart, the devil sees to it that we have the opportunity to become offended. The Scripture that applies to affliction is found in verse 17. It says: *"And have no root in themselves, and so endure but for a time: afterward, when affliction or persecution arises for the word's sake, immediately they are offended."*

This is the parable about sowing seed into different kinds of ground and the predictable success rate at which the seed will sprout and grow. It is a parallel picture from horticulture about what happens when seed is planted or falls into various soils or ground. The seed is the Word of God, and the soil is the condition of the spiritual heart of man. In this verse, we see what happens to someone with a heart that has not allowed a root system to grow. They have just prayed and received a promise. The Word is new to them, and when the pressures of life are applied, they become offended. In the newly converted believer, this is a really easy time to become offended and to let go of the promise. We can be sure that when we take the Word and apply it to a situation, the devil will try to come against us to challenge our faith. He will try to uproot the Word by affliction or persecution right after the seed has been planted in our hearts. He does not want us to develop a root system. This can only develop with time and by protecting the Word that we have received concerning a certain situation.

Afflictions are pressures or weights we allow to torment us. A great majority of Christians read their Bible for knowledge and comfort. I read my Bible to hold my mind and control my emotions in times of affliction. I read the Word to find specific verses that God gives me to stand on. In this way, I use the Word as part of the armor of God for spiritual warfare.

We can use the Word as the sword of the spirit. We do this by reading, keeping the Word in our thinking, and declaring what promises apply to the situation. We can also water the Word in our hearts by studying similar Scriptures or *sister verses*. We can be full of hope knowing that God is always faithful to His Word, and we need to remember not to take affliction personally. In order to not get so devastated by affliction when it comes, it is important to realize that the devil is after the Word in us, not after us personally.

Affliction applies to an individual case whereas the *cares of this world* are on a much larger scale. Famines, epidemics, mass killings, homelessness, abuse to children, are some examples of the *cares of this world*. The homeless plight of one individual or the abuse of one child would be considered an affliction. However, the problem of countless cases of homelessness and large-scale child abuse would fall into the category of the *cares of this world*.

An example of pressures and weights is the case of a single mother trying to make ends meet by working odd jobs to keep food on the table. Poverty is a weight on an individual. A sudden layoff at work is a pressure. More month than money is a real pressure many face daily.

A minister friend of ours told us that there is a process every time we pray. He called it the 3 P's. It's prayer, promise, and pressure. First, we pray for a specific need. Then we receive the promise for that specific need, and then pressure will come. Pressure always comes after the prayer and promise are received. This is where the rubber meets the road in the Christian life. When the test of the devil comes, are we going to allow the plant to be uprooted before we can enjoy its fruit? Are we going to let the devil steal from us those life-giving promises we are entitled to? Or are we going to trust God and His Word?

There are some Scriptures that have helped me during the time I was standing and holding on to the promises of God to manifest. Sometimes all natural evidence will scream at us that we are a fool to believe God. Our minds will ask us what makes us think our circumstances will change? At that time, will we give in or wait patiently for God's promises.

One Scripture that has helped me is Psalm 112:6–8:

"Surely he shall not be moved forever: the righteous shall be in everlasting remembrance. He shall not be afraid of evil tidings: his heart is fixed, trusting in the Lord. His heart is established, he shall not be afraid, until he see his desire upon his enemies."

When I heard this Scripture many years ago, I decided I wanted a heart that would not be afraid and not be moved. It takes plain old determination to hold on to the things of God when the circumstances are contrary to what we have received from His Word. I decided I was not going to be afraid of bad news. I determined to fix my heart and trust in God. I declared that my heart was established and that I would see the destruction of my enemies. I realized that my enemy was the devil, and all his schemes were designed to destroy my trust in God. The devil wants to take our attention away from God. He wants us to establish his kingdom on earth by the words we speak out of our mouths. He wants us to give him the right to live our lives by agreeing with his ways so he will get the glory and not God. He is in the business of getting defectors from God's Kingdom to his kingdom.

I believed God to give me an established heart even though I knew at the time that the situation I was in was a challenge and a stretch for me. But God likes us to reach to His level. When we receive a verse or promise from God, it is His responsibility to establish us. We do not have to have the care or concern of how we will become established. We only need to rest and be assured He will perform it in our hearts in His time as long as we believe and receive from His word that is His will.

Paul said in 2 Corinthians 12:7–10 (NIV):

> *"To keep me from becoming conceited because of these surpassingly great revelations, there was given me a thorn in my flesh, a messenger of Satan, to torment me. Three times I pleaded with the Lord to take it away from me. But he said to me, My grace is sufficient for you, for my power is made perfect in weakness. Therefore I will boast all the more gladly about my weaknesses, so that Christ's power may rest on me. That is why, for Christ's sake, I delight in weaknesses, in insults, in hardships, in persecutions, in difficulties. For when I am weak, then I am strong."*

Paul understood that his troubles were sent to him from the devil. He had a messenger from Satan to provoke the people, to close their hearts, and to cause him all kinds of trouble just to stop the revelation knowledge that Paul preached. On a much smaller scale, we are buffeted by the devil every time we sow a Scripture verse in our hearts. When we make a decision to take God at His Word, we are declaring war against the hosts of hell. We are taking back what is ours by inheritance. We can do as Paul did and remember that when we are at our weakest, that is when God will make us strong. If an affliction can cause us to lean on God during a tough time, then it can bring us the endurance we need to stand against future troubles. We can eventually get to the place where we look at troubles or problems as opportunities to see the power of God work in our lives through His Word.

Another encouraging Scripture is in James 1:2–4:

> *"My brethren, count it all joy when ye fall into divers temptations: Knowing this, that the trying of your faith worketh patience. But let patience have her perfect work, that ye may be perfect and entire, wanting nothing."*

James tells us to count it all joy when we have temptations, tests, and trials. Is that our usual reaction to affliction? Afflictions can come to anyone of us, but we have to know that the trying of our faith will work patience in us. Patience in this case means endurance or consistency. If we endure, we will come to a place of wanting nothing. In a problem situation, we can count it all joy, knowing that this is another opportunity for us to see the Word work on our behalf. We can count it all joy because we know God is in control through our prayers. When we pray His will, the Word will dictate how the problem will be resolved. Through Jesus' work on the cross, we are guaranteed a better covenant. Afflictions have already been defeated by Jesus on the cross. We only need to enforce what He has already done for us. I like the phrase, "We fight from victory, not for victory."

The tests will come in this life, but we do not have to allow them to flatten us. Wanting nothing is a good place of stability to be in God. We are lacking nothing in any situation when we take God at His Word. When we stretch up to God's level, we are raised up to mind the things of the spirit realm, no matter what the natural realm looks like. When we live by the eternal laws, we can transform or change the natural laws to match the eternal ones.

There was a time in our lives when Dennis and I had a fast-food restaurant. Every day we opened, our balance sheet was in the red. Dennis told me that he had the weight of our financial situation so much on his mind that when he went to church, he could not pay attention to the message. Instead of being uplifted and refreshed, he worried about the business failing. During the entire year and a half, we tried to make it work. We were both consumed with the fear of failure and the fear of loss. Because we were still infants in spiritual matters, God gave us a way of escape. He was faithful to move us from Illinois to California and helped us buy and sell two homes within a six-week time frame. He was also faithful to get us out of the restaurant business. It was a disaster. So we took our losses and sold the business. Dennis went back into sales and has been successful ever since. We maintained our trust in God, and that broke the hold that fear had on our minds.

First Corinthians 10:13 was the Scripture that later confirmed to us what happened at that time. The *New International Version* says:

> *"No temptation has seized you except what is common to man. And God is faithful; he will not let you be tempted beyond what you can bear. But when you are tempted, he will also provide a way out, so that you can stand up under it."*

We did not have the spiritual maturity to withstand the devil and live in victory at the time. When this was happening, we were just learning how to take on some spiritual principles and try to live with each other after our separation.

If we cannot stand against the devil in victory by the Word established in our hearts and minds, God will give us a way of escape. He gave me ways of escape many times. I have also seen this way of escape in the lives of women I have counseled. When they were in a mental, physical, or verbally abusive marriage and they continually went under the abuse, God let them separate for a time. This time of separation was used for healing and learning new ways to approach each other. They learned to no longer hinder and hurt each other. We have seen marriages recovered to go on and become wonderful for both parties. There is always the possibility of restoration when a couple looks to God for help.

There is an account in the *New International Version* about Jacob's wives in Genesis 29:16 through 30:24 and continuing in chapter 35:16–18. Laban had two daughters, Leah and Rachel. According to Hebrew custom, the oldest daughter had to marry first, but Jacob wanted to marry the youngest daughter, Rachel. So Jacob promised to serve Laban for seven years if he could marry Rachel. But Laban tricked Jacob and gave him his oldest daughter Leah on his wedding night instead. When Jacob found out it was Leah, he promised to work for Laban another seven years, and he married Rachel one week later. His father-in-law married off both his daughters to Jacob and had fourteen years of free labor from his son-in-law!

In ancient times, these marriages were common. Both sisters had the same husband, but Leah was aware that Jacob loved her sister Rachel more than he loved her. Because of this affliction, she experienced much offense and rejection. Even the Lord saw that she was unloved by Jacob, so He opened her womb and she bore a son, while Rachel remained barren. Leah bore Reuben, which means, "*See a son!*" In verse 29:32, she says, "It is because the Lord has seen my misery. Surely my husband will love me now." Leah had three more sons after Reuben—Simeon, Levi, and Judah. Simeon means *God hears*, Levi means *companion* and Judah means *praise*. She tried so hard to please Jacob and to gain his love. She said in Genesis 29:34, "Now at last my husband will become attached to me, because I have borne him three sons." Leah wanted Jacob to love her as much as he loved Rachel and be her companion more than anything else. If you have ever lived in a marriage where you knew another woman was loved more than you were, you can identify with what Leah felt. It is definitely a situation of affliction! The weight of the torment caused by Jacob's rejection of Leah was tremendous on her.

In the meantime, Rachel saw she had given Jacob no children and her barrenness became an affliction to her. From offense, she goes into envy and then into rejection and hopelessness, which is a symptom of depression. She demands of Jacob out of her state of depression in Genesis 30:1: "*Give me children, or I'll die!*" To end her feelings of rejection and depression, Rachel gives Jacob her maid Bilhah as a secondary wife. Bilhah conceives and births Dan, which means *judged*. There is a second child named Naphtali, which means *struggled*. In Genesis 30:8, Rachel says, "*I have had a great struggle with my sister, and I have a son.*"

The affliction both sisters experienced was caused by the great competition between them. Now Leah, in order to gain ascendancy over her sister, copies Rachel and also gives her maid to Jacob. Two more sons are born. Leah's maid Zilpah birthed Gad, which means *fortune*, and Asher, which means *happy*.

One day, Reuben found some mandrakes during wheat harvest and brought them to his mother, Leah. Mandrakes were superstitiously supposed to excite and win love. Another name for them is love apples. When Rachel heard about it, she asked Leah for some of the mandrakes. In Genesis 30:15–16, Leah made another rejection statement: "*Wasn't it enough that you took away my husband? Will you take my son's mandrakes too?*" So Rachel and Leah made a deal over the mandrakes. The deal was that Leah could go to Jacob's tent that night in return for giving Rachel some mandrakes. These verses seem to imply that Leah was cut off from Jacob and had to get permission from Rachel to sleep with him. God heard Leah's prayer, and she conceived again. Issachar was born, which means *hired*. She was also blessed with another son, Zebulun, which means *honor*. This was her tribute to her husband, as she says in Genesis 30:20, "*God has presented me with a precious gift. This time my husband will treat me with honor, because I have borne him six sons.*"

Leah felt God had given her a good gift for her husband. She thought now he would surely dwell with her and regard her as his wife because she bore him six sons. We do not know if she ever won her husband's affection, but we do know she was blessed by God since the Levites who were the line of the priesthood in Israel came from her son Levi. Jacob may have abandoned Leah, but God was concerned for her continually. The Messiah came from the tribe of Judah also one of Leah's sons.

Rachel had Joseph and another son whom she named Benoni, *son of my sorrow*, for she died giving him life. Jacob changed his name to Benjamin, *son of the right hand*. Leah and Rachel, along with their maidservants, birthed the twelve sons who became the twelve tribes of Israel. For all the affliction, competition, expectation, jealousy, offense, rejection, and depression that the two sisters went through, God brought forth the nation of Israel from their offspring.

As we reflect on affliction in our lives, we must remember that we have a better covenant, and if we can stand for what we know is ours under the covenant that Jesus ratified by His blood, we can walk in consistency and endurance. This can be a blessing to us and a furthering of the Gospel in our lives. When the devil comes to buckle us at the knees, we can speak the Word, thus releasing the faith from our spirit and maintaining our soul at the same time.

Sometimes we live our lives with a victim mentality. We think we have become a victim because of the people in our lives or the circumstances we are going through. Yet it all depends on our perspective and how we see the presence of affliction in our lives. It is up to us. We can take a victimized outlook and feel the full weight of the affliction from the devil or we can decide to count it all joy knowing that the trying of our faith will work consistency, patience, and endurance in us. Thereby we will lack or want nothing.

We can walk in victory whether the situation changes in the natural or not, because we are established on the better promises of the Word. We can know that we have what we have asked for the minute that we ask for it in Jesus' Name. We can know that after having done all to stand, we can stand secure until the victory does come and change our situation in the natural. Whenever we pray, we already have what we prayed in the spiritual realm. We can stand because we keep our minds on the things above and our request has an appointment in the natural realm. Even if it takes years to appear in the natural, the peace of God in our hearts will give us the strength to stand and wait for it knowing we already have the answer to our request. It is just a matter of time before it is manifested here in our lives.

1. Why does affliction come against a believer?

   _____

2. Can affliction be defeated in the believer's life?

   _____

3. How do we defeat the enemy when he uses affliction to stop us?

   _____

4. What kind of affliction did the enemy use to stop Paul?

   _____

5. In this world, will we ever come to a place where there will not be any temptations, tests, and trials?

   _____

6. How can we rely on God in the middle of temptations, tests, and trials?

   _____

7. Why can we count it all joy when we have temptation, tests, and trials?

   _____

CHAPTER 11

Persecution

Mark 4:15–17; Matthew 7:2;
2 Corinthians 10:4–5

In the thesaurus, the synonyms for *persecute* are "abuse, molest, oppress, torture, torment, victimize, harass, heckle and hound." In the dictionary, *persecution* means "to afflict or harass constantly so as to injure or distress; to oppress cruelly, especially for reasons of religion or politics or race."

On the receiving end of persecution, we think we are the victim of our persecutor. We experience harassing and hounding coming at us through their words, and it is definitely a type of oppression. Persecution is also a form of mental and emotional abuse because there is intimidation involved in it as well. If we allow the persecution to take over our minds, we will become intimidated. The fear of man will entrap us because we fear their imagined power over us. We will fear what they can do to us and even what they think of us.

This has happened to me many times, especially when I was sharing the Word of God. Persecution for the Word's sake is when someone attacks us for our beliefs. When this happens, their words can actually injure us if we do not recognize them as persecution. Since it is after the Word in us, we cannot take it personally. I always say this because it is the key to escaping the horrendous hurt of persecution. Do not take it personally. Stay emotionally detached.

In Matthew 7:6 we are warned, *"Do not cast your pearls before swine, lest they trample them under their feet, and turn again and rend you."* Since their words can tear our spirit to pieces, it is not worth it to engage them in an argument because not only will they try to destroy what is precious to us—our *pearls*—but they will also try to injure our person. We may end up being torn and injured. *Rending* implies a deep fatal wound to our viscera, or insides, and is something difficult to recover from.

Persecutions for the Word's sake or *persecution* in the Bible is usually instigated by Satan to challenge the Word in us. He will bring the persecution to us through people. If we are established in our belief in some truth, it should not matter what people think of us. But it is when we are not so sure of what we believe that we will become a target of the enemy. He will send people to challenge our beliefs. We will have to ask ourselves what we believe. Even though it feels threatening when it happens, it can be a positive experience in that it will cause us to clarify our beliefs, and our position will be strengthened.

Mark 4:15–17 says:

> *"And these are they by the wayside where the word is sown and when they have heard, Satan comes immediately to take the word that was sown in their hearts. And these are they who likewise were sown on stony ground, who when they have heard the word immediately receive it with gladness and have no root in themselves so endure but for a time. Afterward, when affliction and persecution arises for the word's sake, immediately they are offended."*

Here we have two hearts: a *wayside* heart and a *stony-ground* heart. One has heard the Word, and the other has heard and received the Word with gladness, but both have no root system yet. So they will endure only for a short time. They endure only as long as life is wonderful. If we catch ourselves enduring for only a short time and then falling away, we have to bring our minds back by saying to ourselves, "I refuse to have a wayside heart. I refuse to have a stony heart. I have a good-ground heart with a root system, and everything I receive from the Word of God is true." This is the way to counteract the enemy when he tries to steal the Word from our hearts. Every time we want to grow in some revelation in the Word, it requires a decision of our will. With the decision in order to become established with a root system in our heart, there needs to be diligence, determination, discipline, and declaration of the truth we have received in seed form from the Word of God.

Once the decision is made and the root system is started, we guard and water the seed with like Scriptures. The establishing of our thinking is done in the soul. Again Jesus already bought and paid for our success in the Word. We enforce this truth by speaking to ourselves and saying, "Soul, you will think and act in line with the Word of God." This should not sound strange to us when we consider how much effort professional athletes put into mastering their disciplines. Even the Olympic Games participants speak to their bodies when they train them. Since spiritual warfare targets our mind to control it, we must discipline our thoughts. We, as soldiers in the Lord's army, cannot be lazy in the mental and spiritual realm. We must understand the training we need to undergo in order to do spiritual warfare.

I spent many years questioning my belief in God, especially when the teaching I presented in the weekly Bible study was challenged. When my teaching was challenged, it would shake me and I would doubt the teaching for a short time while I questioned God again about it. But I finally realized that this was persecution in the form of a challenge, and it was directed toward the Word in me and not personally at me. I simply could not take it personally. I learned to go back to God with my beliefs and to turn the persecution into a time of renewed teaching and receiving from God. I determined that if what I believed was the truth, it would carry me through. If not, I needed to change my thinking anyway.

One of the reasons Christians buckle under persecution is that they wish it was not happening to them. They whimper, resist, and wonder why this is happening instead of accepting it as a way of life and realizing that persecution is part of the Christian life and it will be with us as long as we are on this earth. But we must remember that God has given us enough grace in every persecution to endure and the strength to respond the way Jesus would have instead of reacting in our flesh when we are challenged.

Persecution is also one of the high things that exalts itself against the knowledge of God mentioned in 2 Corinthians 10:4–5. We read:

> *For the weapons of our warfare are not carnal, but mighty through God to the pulling down of strong holds: Casting down imaginations, and every high thing that exalteth itself against the knowledge of God, and bringing into captivity every thought to the obedience of Christ . . .*

When persecution came at me and I took it personally, it became a high thing in my mind. It was so high that it took over all my thoughts, and I became obsessed and focused on the persecution. I spent my whole day in speculation. I became self-centered. I rehearsed over and over mentally what was said to me, and I was offended again and again. Then I felt rejected and sorry for myself. I thought to myself, *Why did I ever teach such a controversial subject to my Bible group?*

When we let the high things exalt themselves, we become center stage in our thinking instead of letting God be on the throne. Take the teaching to Him and say, "Is this what you want me to believe? Take me through this again and give me scriptural confirmation that this is what you want me to teach." Then His answer will come. He is faithful to let us know, and at this point, we have to be all right with it. If we anchor our minds and emotions in the Word, then we should not care what people say. When God has revealed to us where He wants our thinking, we can endure any persecution.

If we get offended and upset with those bringing the persecution, we are reacting like our heart is a wayside heart or a stony-ground heart without a root system. If we do not have any root system in what we say or what we believe in, we will not be able to endure very long when we are challenged.

Persecution is also designed to attack our faith level and rob us of our peace. So if there are false and railing accusations coming against us and we are going under them mentally or emotionally, then we are being offended at what is being said about us or to us.

Lamentations 5:1–5 talks about Judah and Jerusalem. You can hear the offense and rejection in their words:

> *"Remember, O Lord, what is come upon us: consider, and behold our reproach. Our inheritance is turned to strangers, our houses to aliens. We are orphans and fatherless, our mothers are as widows. We have drunken our water for money; our wood is sold unto us. Our necks are under persecution: we labor, and have no rest."*

This is a picture of what Judah and Jerusalem went through. This passage continues to say that they were slaves in Egypt and Assyria. Their women and children suffered to the point where they had no honor or joy left in their hearts, yet they brought these persecutions on themselves. They eventually endured the persecution from the people who attacked them and came against them. Verses 20–22:

> *"Wherefore dost Thou forget us forever, and forsake us so long time? Turn Thou us unto Thee, O Lord, and we shall be turned; renew our days as of old. But Thou hast utterly rejected us; Thou art very wroth against us."*

The people of Judah and Jerusalem thought they were utterly forsaken by God. With persecution comes the outlook that focuses on what we do not have instead of what we do have. It focuses on what has been taken from us instead of what we still have. When we are experiencing persecution, it is easy to feel "woe is me" and to ask ourselves, "Why is this happening to me?" We see only what has been taken from us. We see only the negatives in our lives instead of the blessings that are still there, and this is a fertile environment for resentment and self-pity the enemy capitalizes on.

In Matthew 5:11 we read:

> *Blessed are you when men shall revile you and perse-cute you and shall say all manner of evil against you falsely, for my name's sake. Rejoice and be exceeding glad for great is your reward in heaven, for so perse-cuted they the prophets which were before you.*

Persecution is not new. Countless numbers of Christians have endured persecution over the centuries. Persecution came to Jesus. It also came to all of the prophets. But it can be especially hard to deal with when persecution comes to us from family members or fellow believers.

> *"You have heard that it has been said that thou shalt love thy neighbor and hate thy enemy, but I say unto you, love your enemies and bless them that curse you. Do good to them that hate you and pray for them that despitefully use you and persecute you." (Matt. 5:43–48)*

These are instructions to us from the Lord to help our thinking when we experience persecution. Jesus was persecuted, and He did not even open His mouth in self-defense.

First Peter 2:20 says:

> *"For what glory is it when you be buffeted for your faults, you shall take it patiently? But if when you do well and suffer for it, you take it patiently, that*

is acceptable with God. Even were you called to this because Christ also suffered for us leaving us an example that you should follow His steps; who did no sin, neither was guile found in His mouth; who, when He was reviled, reviled not again; when He suffered, He threatened not, but committed Himself to Him who judges righteously."

Buffeted means to be beat up or given blows with the hand or fist, to get in a fight or a struggle over our actions. When we are caught for doing wrong and we are beat up for it, we will feel some pressure but we can understand it because, after all, we did the wrong. But when we have done nothing wrong, but in fact have done a good deed, and we are still buffeted, that is hard to understand or take patiently. We must look to Jesus as our example and forerunner. If He did not open His mouth in self-defense when He was innocent, we can rely on Him in us to take our persecution patiently. Of course, that means we have to die to *self* because *self* wants to rise up in righteous indignation. *Self* wants to defend itself. But remember that taking persecution patiently is acceptable behavior with God.

It helps to realize that we will never be rejected to the degree that Jesus was rejected nor have the opportunities to be offended as He had. Yet He did not sin as a result of His persecution. We will probably never have whole armies after us, as David had, trying to kill us. So we can take comfort in this knowledge. But now we have the warfare in the spirit. We already have authority over the enemy in both the natural and in the spirit realm, but we have to learn to fight back in the spirit, not in our flesh.

The light of God is seen in us whether we think it is or not. It is seen by the people of the world, and it can offend them because they think godliness is foolishness. The natural mind, according to 1 Corinthians 2:14 says that man's wisdom and knowledge is foolishness. I would much rather have God as my source of wisdom and knowledge and not the world. I would much rather be in a relationship with Jesus and the God of this universe than with people, especially people with a worldly mentality. Do not be afraid to continue to speak for God. This is who we are, a child of His. When we take up our cross and follow Him, we are putting down our flesh and the thinking we learned from the world. This means putting down our natural reactions, our reasoning, and the thinking that has been too familiar and common for us.

There is a way to walk in victory when there are accusations and persecutions coming against us. I have shared these Scriptures earlier, but they have worked and continue to work for me. Maybe the Holy Spirit will give you completely different verses to help you, but they will be yours and that is what counts. You can pray like I did, "Thank You, Father. Who can charge anything to the elect of God? It is God that justifies. Thank you, Father, I'm justified in this situation. I receive my vindication. And I receive that all things hidden come to light, that all the right people will know what is the truth, in Jesus' Name." This prayer contains Scriptures from Romans 8:33 and Mark 4:22. Since we are already justified in the spirit realm, let us receive our justification in the natural realm also.

Romans 8:31 says, *"And what shall you say to these things. If God be for you, who can be against you?"* After this prayer, we do what we need to do each day to keep ourselves calm and in a place of peace. When the situation arises in our thinking, we must remind ourselves of our prayer and keep receiving God's peace for the situation. If we have to confront an accusation, we can pray the Scripture in Matthew 10:19–20:

> *"But when they deliver you up, take no thought on what you or how you shall speak, for it shall be given you in the same hour what you shall speak. For it is not you that speaks, but the Spirit of the Father that speaks in you."*

This Scripture prepares us and settles us. We do not have to have any anxiety or mental striving over what we will say. God will give us the words to say when the time comes.

A friend of mine experienced the persecution mind trap when her grown daughter moved to New York and began spending a lot of time with her aunt who lived there. Almost every conversation my friend had on the phone with her, the daughter accused her falsely. The mother found herself offended and rejected when she hung up. Every time the mother tried to defend herself from her daughter's accusations, she felt she missed the grace of God. She missed the grace of God by becoming offended, instead of putting down her flesh, she wanted to defend herself. God wanted her to be patient and wait on Him. She had to let her daughter see the truth about her aunt for herself. We read earlier that Jesus did not open his mouth to defend Himself when He was reviled and He was innocent.

The result was what my friend called a *glory day* when her daughter called her up and told her of an incident. Her aunt invited her to a fancy restaurant for dinner in New York City. Her uncle was out of town, and her aunt wanted to see her. The niece told her aunt that she had already made plans for that evening and that she could not meet her, but her aunt would not take no for an answer. Her aunt said, "How dare you not meet me for dinner when I just took you to London and bought you a brand-new full length winter coat! Are you going to tell me you can't come to dinner with me when your uncle is out of town and I'm free?" My friend's daughter said, "Yes, that's exactly what I'm telling you because I've been invited out by a family I know and I already have plans."

When my friend had tried to tell her daughter four years before how controlling her aunt was, her daughter became offended and said, "How dare you say that about my aunt? She's not controlling. She's just trying to help me." When she tried to warn her daughter about her aunt, the Lord told her to be quiet and said to her, "That's My job." My friend forgave her sister in New York for all the control she had exercised on her in the past while they were growing up, and she repented for gossiping against her. While she waited on the Lord, her daughter came to the realization about her aunt by herself. She had to keep quiet for four years before this *glory day* happened, but it was well worth the wait. She had the grace of God during that time to control herself. She dealt with her emotional baggage in her heart toward her sister, and she had victory over her habit of gossiping about her.

1.   When persecution comes at us, what is its purpose?

     _____

2.   What did Jesus do when people persecuted Him?

     _____

3.   How should we judge persecution?

     _____

4.   What does persecution try to do to us emotionally?

     _____

     When we recognize this _____, forgive them
     and ourselves.

5.   How can we walk in victory when accusations and perse-
     cutions come against us?

     _____

6.   What is the best way to confront accusation?

     _____

7.   What is the benefit of Romans 8:31?

     _____

CHAPTER 12

Cares of This World

Matthew 11:28–30;
1 Peter 5:5–6; Philippians 4:6–7

In the thesaurus, the synonyms for *care* are "worry, anxiety and distress." In the dictionary *cares* are defined as "a troubled or burdened state of mind, worry, concern; suggests a weighing down of the mind as by dread, apprehension or great responsibility."

The *cares* of this world are around us daily. Our news media keeps us supplied with an ongoing, horrendous outpouring of events that is guaranteed to make us worry and fill us with fear. This mind trap consumes our thinking as we fret or become anxious over our own situations or with those around us.

I can remember the exact place I was standing when I realized Satan was the one bringing every care, worry, and concern to me. The cares and worries he brought were designed to choke the Word of God that I had hidden in my heart. He knew that if he could keep me upset with the affairs of life, I would not be a threat to him. When I realized care, worry, and concern were his work, I made a decision to become an intercessor instead of a worrier. Instead of being taken captive by his schemes to worry, I prayed for each situation in my life and for those around me. When I knew what the will of God was for me and for them, I prayed accordingly.

Let's look at the right thinking or positive side of *cares*. This type of *care* is ministering love to those in need. An example of this is in Deuteronomy 32:10:

> *"He found him in a desert land, and in the waste howling wilderness; he led him about, he instructed him, he kept him as the apple of his eye. As an eagle stirreth up her nest, fluttereth over her young, spreadeth abroad her wings, taketh them, beareth them on her wings: So the Lord alone did lead him, and there was no strange god with him."*

In this passage, God finds Jacob in the desert. It is a picture of provision and God's tender care for Jacob. God's care is compared to how a mother eagle cares for her young. The young eaglets are completely dependent on her, and she meets their every need. When we are dependent on God's care, as the young eaglets are on their mother, He alone will lead us and protect us.

Another example of ministering love or the positive side of *cares* is found in Genesis 39:6. Joseph was the caretaker for the estate of Potiphar, the Egyptian army captain. As caretaker, Joseph had the stewardship responsibilities over Potiphar's land and all his possessions. Even with the trouble that Potiphar's wife caused Joseph and the suffering of spending years in prison, he was eventually elevated to the second highest position under Pharaoh in all of Egypt. This showed God's caring hand throughout Joseph's life.

There are many different names for Jehovah: Jehovah Jireh, Jehovah Shalom, Jehovah Ropheka, and Jehovah Nissi, to name just a few. They are all different faces of God and show different aspects of His character. He is the God who will see and provide, the God who is our peace, the God who is our healer, and the God who is a banner over us. All these attributes of God show us how He took care of Jacob. God was to Jacob whatever he needed in each situation. But Jacob also gave place to God. He was upright before Him throughout his life and built altars to Him. Jacob received God's favor because he responded to Him. Throughout the Bible, we see that we have a God who cares for us and wants to meet all our needs.

Genesis 2:15 says, *"And God took man and put him in the Garden of Eden to work it and take care of it."* Not only does God want to take care of us, He wants us to take care of what is ours. We are to be good stewards over our homes and lands, our children, and all our possessions that God gives us. Some of these possessions, like our children, are merely on loan to us for a few years, but we are co-laborers with God in their lives for that designated time. As far as our material possessions go, such as furniture, when we dust and vacuum our homes we are being caretakers or stewards over those things. We do the work because the things mean something and have value to us and we love them. By caring for them, we show our love for them. This is on the positive side of *cares of this world.*

On the negative side of *cares of this world*, there is a weighing down in the mind or a troubled and burdened state of mind. In Genesis 21:11–12 there is an example of Abraham when he was greatly distressed because of Ishmael. But God said to him, *"Do not be so distressed about the boy or your maid servant, it is through Isaac that your offspring will be reckoned."* At the time, Abraham was greatly distressed about sending Hagar and Ishmael away in the desert, but God was faithful and made a covenant with them to take care of them.

Martha got caught in this mind trap when Jesus came to her house in Bethany. The story is found in Luke 10:38–42:

> *"Now it came to pass, as they went, that he entered into a certain village: and a certain woman named Martha received him into her house. And she had a sister called Mary, which also sat at Jesus' feet, and heard his word. But Martha was cumbered about much serving, and came to him, and said. Lord, dost thou not care that my sister hath left me to serve alone? Bid her therefore that she help me. And Jesus answered and said unto her, Martha, Martha, thou*

art careful and troubled about many things: But one thing is needful: and Mary hath chosen that good part, which shall not be taken away from her."

"Mary hath chosen that good part" could be paraphrased, *"Mary has chosen the better way."* On the other hand, we see Martha being overly concerned about preparing and serving the meal. She became offended when Mary left the kitchen to sit at Jesus' feet to listen to Him. She felt neglected and overwhelmed. She allowed the work to consume her mind instead of keeping the tasks in the natural in subjection to the spiritual. If we keep God's peace and order in every situation, we can keep these things from lording it over us. We can keep them in their right perspective.

In any situation when we find ourselves harassed or over-whelmed, we must recognize that it is the devil bringing us all the stress, pressure, and tension. It all depends on the way we choose to see or perceive the situation. If it is a mental thought harassing us, we can stop and say, "I resist this pressure and I thank you, Father, that I have the mind of Christ in this situation, in Jesus' Name." If it is a task that seems overwhelming, we can stop and say, "I have authority over this project and I thank you, Father, you are able to open up ways of accomplishing it." We will be able to handle it. We can also say, "Stress, pressure, and tension, you have no part of my thinking. You are under my feet, in Jesus' Name. I thank you, Father, I have the right kind of thinking in this situation."

Being overwhelmed and feeling pressured comes from the devil, and both have their own thought process behind them. They are not part of God's plan for our lives. By stopping and praying, we can take authority over the situation and put ourselves back in the head position instead of the tail position. It does not have to take us more than a minute to get control over whatever is disturbing and over-whelming us. Remember, God promised us an abundant life. These things should not be lording over us.

There are many Scripture verses that show us pictures of the neg-ative effects of worry and care in our lives. All these verses have words such as *very concerned, fearful,* or *distressed* in them. In Numbers 22:3 it says, *"The land of Moab was very distressed and afraid of the people."* Psalm 37:8 says, *"Cease from anger and forsake wrath, fret not thyself in any wise to do evil."* Once offended in our anger we want to retaliate and not have any other people get away with evil. We think they are accomplishing things while we are not effective because we are being upright, honest, and faithful to God.

We are to not fret ourselves or be concerned about others. Their day is coming. There is a price they will have to pay for their work. When there is sowing to evil, there will be reaping to evil in their lives. Because we do not see it, does not mean that it is not going to happen. Besides, we are not looking for somebody to pay us back and expect them to return to us what they stole or took from us. Just forgive them and let them go free. When we forgive them, we set them free to receive what is justly theirs, and if we really forgave them, we will not look for justice to come to them and consequences to come to them. Let the Lord take care of them and leave them with Him. Let Him be God. He will have mercy on them just as He has had mercy on us.

In Psalm 55:22 it says, *"Cast your burden upon the Lord, He will sustain thee: he shall never suffer the righteous to be moved."* Psalm 94:19 reads, *"When anxiety was great within, your consolation brought joy to my soul."* His Word will dispel fear and replace it with joy. We can get all the natural knowledge that both secular and religious institutions and support groups can offer us, but the only thing that creates life within us and brings us real results is the Word of God.

Another Scripture about *cares* is found in Luke 21:34. It says, *"Be careful or your hearts will be weighed down with dissipation, drunkenness and the anxieties of life and that day will close on you unexpectedly like a trap."* So we have to be watchful, and we are to be smart. When the anxieties of life come at us or we read the situations in the newspaper or hear it on TV, we are not to take it in. We have to go immediately into intercession because by praying the answer for someone else, we can protect our own souls from being taken over by the care and anxiety of their situation.

Remember, words bring the thoughts, thoughts bring the images, and the images can strike fear in our hearts. If we take the image of fear, Satan has another seed that he can harvest in our lives. We have to guard ourselves and our reactions against fear-filled words and images.

One of the most vivid examples of this came when the space shuttle Challenger exploded seventy-three seconds after liftoff on January 28, 1986. All seven astronauts on board were killed. It was a major disaster for our country. There was so much publicity leading up to the event, and the launch was televised. This was the first time a teacher was going into space. Christa McAuliffe's family and her whole classroom of students were watching. I watched the liftoff on TV, and when the shuttle exploded, I saw the shock and devastation on the faces of the teacher's family and her students. The moment was filled with terror, disbelief, and grief. All I could do was to start praying for everyone I could think of to hold myself together. I was so moved. When I start to feel myself get shaky about something, I go immediately into prayer. That is my survival mode. I just keep talking to God and talking to myself in prayer until I again find a place of rest for my soul.

The shuttle disaster must have occurred on a Wednesday because it was the night of our midweek church service. When I got to church, many had taken the care of the situation on themselves and were grieving inconsolably. If I had said anything to them about being under the care of the situation, they would have become offended. It is better to show compassion and take authority over the devil's words and tactics as an intercessor on their behalf separate from the emotion at the time. Otherwise, people become offended because they think we do not care.

Not getting under the care of a situation is to understand that the most effective thing we can do is pray. It is not that we have no compassion for the pain that the people are experiencing in the situation, but we pray to ensure that the care of the situation does not consume our whole thinking. Most people confuse sympathy with compassion and are drawn into the crises with their emotions to the point of going under the care. At that point, they are ineffective as intercessors in the spiritual realm since they are in their emotions.

Many Christians practice the verse, "Bear one another's burdens," but they bear them carnally or with their natural minds and emotions. That is natural sympathy and pity and cannot help others spiritually. Many codependent people love to wallow in other people's problems and get overwhelmed by them so they do not have to face their own issues and straighten out their own chaotic lives. The Holy Spirit is always there waiting to help, but they have forsaken their own mercy.

I want to be able to hear God at all times, but the *cares of this world* is the way the devil puts the weight of the world on my shoulders to shut my ears. When I go under this mind trap, I take on false responsibility and false burden that God has not equipped me to carry. When the *cares of this world* enter into my mind, they choke God's Word. My thinking is consumed, and the Holy Spirit has to wait for me to get tired of carrying the whole load by myself. He has to wait until I am ready to let go of it and can roll it over onto Him.

Jesus said in Matthew 11:28–30:

> *"Come unto me, all ye that labour and are heavy laden, and I will give you rest. Take my yoke upon you, and learn of me: for I am meek and lowly in heart: and ye shall find rest unto your souls. For my yoke is easy, and my burden is light."*

Paul reminds us in 1 Peter 5:5–6 of His promise to us:

> *"Humble yourselves therefore under the mighty hand of God, that he may exalt you in due time: Casting all your care upon him; for he careth for you."*

These are two of my favorite Scriptures I use when an opportunity to take on false responsibility and false burden presents itself. Jesus never wants me to lose my soul rest, but it is up to me to keep words, thoughts, and images out of my soul by rolling the care of them over onto Him. His shoulders are big enough, and His promises are good enough to match any stressful situation.

1. What should we do when we recognize the pressures of life are attacking us?

   _____

2. Where does the believer receive the cares of the world in their daily lives?

   _____

3. How can we combat fear and terror?

   _____

4. How do we help those around us when they are caught up in the care of a situation?

   _____

5. Name two traits that come with the cares of this world.

   _____

6. What purpose does the enemy have by using the cares of this world?

   _____

Deceitfulness of Riches

Mark 4:19; Proverbs 13:7–8, 18; Philippians 1:6;
Proverbs 10:22

In the thesaurus, the synonyms for *deceit* are "false, crafty, cunning, beguiling, misleading, devious, deceptive and fraudulent." The dictionary says *deceive* implies "deliberate misrepresentation of facts by words and actions, generally to further one's end." The devil uses deceit as a deliberate misrepresentation of the facts.

To *mislead* is "to cause to follow the wrong course or to err in conduct or action," and *beguile* implies "the use of wiles and enticing prospects and ways of deceiving or misleading."

Without the deception of the devil, riches can have a positive side in our thinking. We read that God sees His people as His peculiar treasure, and He is willing to bless and enrich them. In Exodus 19:5 it says: *"Now therefore if you will obey my voice indeed and keep my covenant, then you shall be a peculiar treasure unto Me above all people for all the earth is mine."*

We know that this passage is talking about Israel, God's covenant people. Since we are in Christ and He is the guarantee of a better covenant, we know any blessings belong to us too. In Deuteronomy 28:12, it reads:

"The Lord shall open unto thee His good treasure, the heaven to give the rain unto thy land in his season and to bless all the work of thy hand. And thou shalt lend unto many nations and thou shalt not borrow."

The Lord shall open up His treasure to us. From these two verses, we see that we are God's peculiar treasure and He will open His treasures up to us. If we have any treasure or wealth, God is the source of it. Everything we have received came from Him. God is not withholding anything from us. And if we walk in His precepts and His principles, His blessings will be there for us. The riches get thrown in as part of the bargain! It is not that we do things because we are looking for riches, but it is because our hearts are established, and we want to be a blessing to people.

There are two sides to *deceitfulness of riches*. On one side is a grandiose mentality where every thought is about how money, success, and power go hand in hand. These are usually the thoughts of materialistic people who trust in riches. They place their self-worth on the amount of *things* they have accumulated. These people say, "Look at all my possessions. I'm a self-made man. Look at all I've accomplished!" But in God's eyes, they have nothing! The things they prize so highly are worthless! They are not going to take them with them when they die. In Luke 12:15 Jesus said: *"Watch out. Be on guard against all kinds of greed. A man's life does not consist in the abundance of his possessions."*

Very well said! For not even when one has an abundance of material goods does his life consist in the abundance of his possessions. There had better be more than possessions because things are not going to fix the emptiness in our hearts that only God can fill.

The one who has a humble spirit with the right outlook on life is rich in God's eyes. A man who knows the value of things and who knows that he has nothing except what he receives from God has great riches. He has the right attitude in his thinking. He gives God the credit for everything he has and not himself. Besides the blessings we have in God here on earth, we will receive a reward in heaven.

With the right attitude in our thinking, we can store up abundant riches. God is to be our riches, and we can take that all the way to the jewels in our crown! If we have lived our lives and our own heart does not condemn us, we have riches. We have great wealth around us when we are not condemned, and one of the greatest riches is peace of mind. I find to have peace of mind is truly great wealth in this world.

The devil beguiles and entices us with promises of a fortune. He is bringing thoughts and words that form deceitful images. It is to further his gain and his kingdom. He wants his ends to be met, not ours. He distracts us from the Word and from being diligent with long hours of watching TV, talking on the phone, or anything he can use. He makes sin look rosy and easy. But sin always has some form of bondage connected with it. That is why I refuse to be the devil's puppet on a string or have a silver ring in my nose anymore. I did that for years, and now I am free from his bondage. I am glad I have the picture of a puppet or silver ring within me. It helps to keep my thinking constant on Him and not be my own worst enemy.

In grandiose thinking, the devil beguiles us with promises of having a fortune or entices us with hopes of winning some sweepstakes. Chasing rainbows would be a description of the deceit he uses to trap our minds to crave riches. Some people even play the lottery believing God will cause them to win so they can buy a house, pay their bills, and become financially secure and independent. Their faith is in the riches, and riches become their god.

We actually knew a couple who once played a McDonald's sweepstakes game, believing God that they would win. They put a hundred dollars toward the down payment on a house. They were hoping God would have them win the sweepstakes so they could pay the rest of the down payment. After doing this, they came to us for counseling. I asked, "If you were not a Christian, would you put a sum of money down on a house knowing you can't come up with the rest of it?" They said no. Then I said to them, "Whether you are a Christian or not and whether you live by faith or not, you have to have the money first." The error they made was to trust in money to change their life.

This is very much like addiction to drugs or alcohol. It is not the drug or alcohol in itself that is the problem, it is the person's dependence on the substance to make them something other than what they are. They are looking to the substance for a way out of their feelings about themselves or a situation.

Riches and possessions cannot be our priority. The proper progression has to be that we are financially secure in God first, then our needs will be met. In buying a house, we need to have the down payment for it. We must have the means to make the monthly payments, and we must have the credit rating that will get us a mortgage or loan. All these things should be in place. This is a classic example of how deceitfulness of riches takes people captive.

My thinking was exposed in this area when we decided it was time to sell our business and for Dennis to go back into a sales position. I thought if he could acquire a job with a weekly salary, like he had before, we would be secure. I was in front of the fireplace in the living room one day when I realized that my faith was in the weekly salary, not in God.

I also found myself mentally striving over Christmas presents one year. I was warring in my mind to keep purchases under a certain amount so we would have money left over for a *just in case*. I was also offended at the way I had to juggle the amount of money spent on each family member. My reliance was back on money and wishing I had a large windfall. Was my trust in God as my source? No. The worst part was that God had already taught me by the direction of the Holy Spirit and the inward witness in my spirit how to make my purchases years before this incident. At that time, I was faithful to consult Him. I surveyed the newspaper and watched for sales, and I checked with Dennis on major purchases. This was how I shopped. I just followed the peace in my heart, and I made it through the Christmas season and within my budget. Anyway, my pouting stopped when Dennis told me I was walking in *deceitfulness of riches*.

This was when I learned that *deceitfulness of riches* can work not only on the grandiose side but also on the poverty side. Poverty thinking sounds like this: "If we buy this now, we will not have enough money later." Thinking this way finds us always coming up short, never having enough to meet our needs, and it leads to constant mental striving and bondage. If we first consult God and survey all our means, then when we enter into buying something, we are doing it in faith and the means for meeting our needs as they come up will always be there.

Finally, I got to the point that I realized my needs were already met! Yes, I repented and bound *deceitfulness of riches* from operating through me in Jesus' Name. I again followed my heart and believed God that all my needs would be met today, tomorrow, and always. I realized no matter when I go to the Word for a particular Scripture, it will always say the same thing. It is never going to change. I could either stay in poverty thinking or believe in the abundant life. It was up to me to choose when I went to the Word to believe and receive what God's Word said to me.

The rich young ruler in Scripture is an example of how riches can hold the mind.

Luke 18:22–25 says:

> *"And Jesus said unto him. You lack in one thing. Sell all you have. Distribute to the poor and thou shalt have treasure in heaven. When he heard this he was very sorrowful, for he was very rich. And when Jesus saw that he became very sorrowful, He said, How hard it is for those who have riches to enter the kingdom of God! For it is easier for a camel to go through the eye of a needle than for a rich man to enter the kingdom of God."*

Jesus told the rich young ruler to sell all he had and distribute it to the poor, but he became very sorrowful. That is a rejection statement. His priorities were in the wrong place. We can have riches, but they cannot have us. We always have to have an open hand to be able to distribute everything. Nothing in our home or among our possessions should mean so much to us that we cannot give them away.

Another example of an entrapment of our thinking is when we have a blessing come to us, but we get sorrowful about it. There is a

Scripture in Proverbs 10:22 that helps keep my soul. It reads, *"The blessing of the Lord, it maketh rich, and he addeth no sorrow with it."* Sometimes when we have increased riches in our home or our job, we want to go back to what we had before and what was familiar to us. When we do this, we miss our blessing today by allowing sorrow to enter into our present blessing. It is another way for the devil to have us live in the past instead of enjoying and possessing the blessings in the present. Sometimes, we think we do not deserve the new position or we have a bittersweet experience because someone lost the job that we were hired for. But it is not our position in God to take on someone else's life situation. If we get hired and someone gets fired to make a place for us, we can pray God's blessing and provision into their life and thereby not take on false responsibility for their being let go. We cannot allow these distorted kinds of thinking steal the enjoyment of today's blessings from us.

In Mark 4:19 we read, *"The cares of this world and the deceitfulness of riches and the lusts of other things entering in, choke the Word and it becomes unfruitful."* I have always seen this parable to mean that these wiles of the devil can enter into our soul or into our thinking. When we take these as images into our minds, we become double-minded. Then the Word of God cannot come up from our hearts to our minds, and it becomes unfruitful. When afflictions, persecutions, cares of this world, deceitfulness of riches or lusts of other things enter in and fill our minds, it chokes out the Word and it dies.

It is the same with anything that comes from the devil. When he lies and deceives us, we choke the Word in our hearts and we can't hold our minds. We become double-minded. We have two kinds of thinking going on in our minds, and we are listening to two different voices. One is coming from our heart and is saying the things that line up with the Word of God. The other one is saying the opposite, and it will be self-centered. *Deceitfulness of riches* is one way of thinking that enters in and chokes the Word. When we go off the Word and have ourselves a pity party, we will go around and around in our thinking for a time. Eventually, we will have to come back and take up the Word again. These round trips are a waste of time and energy. We are going to have to go back and find where we left off with the

Lord, remember the promise and continue from there. The only positive is every trip we take in our thinking is a round trip.

The following verses describe the many characteristics of poverty thinking:

- *Laziness* – Proverbs 10:4 says, *"He becometh poor that deals with a slack hand, but the hand of the diligent makes rich."*

- *Destruction* – Proverbs 10:15 says, *"The rich man's wealth is his strong city, the destruction of the poor is their poverty."*

- *Hoarding* – Proverbs 11:24 says, *"There is one who scatters and yet increases all the more, and one who withholds what is justly due, but it results only in poverty."*

If we give our belongings or the things that we do not need to the poor, we are scattering and that is eventually going to bring increase to us according to this verse. Withholding more than is necessary is hoarding and leads to poverty. Some people are hoarding all kinds of things. Are we saving broken parts that we may use someday? If we become a saver with a *just-in-case* mentality, we could end up with ten thousand parts that do not fit anything!

God is not wasteful. There are things that we should save, but then there are things that are broken and should be discarded. Maybe we will use them and maybe we will not, but it may all just pile up and be good for nothing. Ask God what He wants us to keep and what He wants us to throw away, and then get rid of it! And why not exercise your faith to believe God for the money to buy new items?

- *Not Teachable and Shame* – Proverbs 13:7–8 reads:

   "There is that makes himself rich yet has nothing.
   There is that makes himself poor yet has great riches.
   The ransom of a man's life are his riches and the
   poor hears not rebuke."

Verse 13:18 reads:

> *Poverty and shame shall be to him that refuses instruction, but he that regards reproof shall be honored.*

Usually, someone who is in poverty will not take correction from anyone. They will not hear rebuke. They do not really want to change their ways or clean up their act. The result of not being teachable concerning poverty will be shame since they will not hear rebuke and they refuse instruction.

- *Lack of Judgment and Laziness* – Proverbs 13:23 reads, *"Much food is in the tillage of the poor but there is that is destroyed for want of judgment."*

Here is a picture of the price of poverty thinking. Their laziness keeps them from cultivating or working their land, so it is left untilled without a crop. Fallow land is useless and unproductive. Those with this thinking lack judgment, stewardship, and management skills. Also, there is very little willingness to work. Because of very little foresight, they might even have an abundance of food but it is for today only. The groceries are for that day. They do not shop for groceries for a week at a time. The Bible says poverty and shame shall be to him that refuses instruction. In my counseling experience, I found this same pattern of deceit time after time. They heard the suggestions but were really looking for a hand out to cure the present crisis. We decided to not be in the Band-Aid business and to not give a hand out if it fed the person's problem and kept them in poverty. If giving them assistance with food or rent was needed and it did not feed poverty thinking, we would help. Those in leadership positions in ministries have to watch out for the *Freddy Freeloaders* out there who just want a handout. There is a saying "Don't give a fish; teach them to fish." If they are not teachable, let them go their way.

From another perspective, we cannot be productive Christians and be lazy. We cannot be lazy in appropriating the blessings of God and holding on to them. We cannot be lazy in spiritual warfare and in living the *more than a conqueror's* life. We are responsible to walk in the knowledge we have been given regarding God's provisions. And it is our responsibility to appropriate those provisions, keeping God as our source of supply.

- *Priorities out of order* – Proverbs 21:17 says, *"He that loves pleasure shall be a poor man, he that loves wine and oil shall not be rich."*

We must keep our priorities in order. If they are not in order, we will pay by falling into poverty thinking. Pleasure and having fun are not the problems here. We can have and should participate in fun activities with family and friends. But with poverty thinking there are no boundaries and no limits, only extremes. We cannot be foolish and show no judgment. If we want to eat, we have to work. We all have to be diligent with what God has given us. He has made us to be stewards over everything we possess.

- *Unwise spending habits* – Proverbs 21:20 says, *"There is treasure to be desired and oil in the dwelling of the wise, but the foolish spends it up."*

In other words, if we have unwise spending habits, we will waste the resources God has given us. There will always be holes in our pockets where the money runs out.

- *Uncleanness and contempt for government* – Ephesians 4:19 reads, *"Who being past feeling have given themselves over to lasciviousness, to work all uncleanness with greediness."*

2 Peter 2:10 reads, *"But chiefly them that walk after the flesh in the lust of uncleanness and despise government."*

We are not to live as the heathen in their perverseness. This lifestyle of perverseness and practicing excess to the point that is past feeling is a sign of not being teachable. Wherever there is order, people in poverty mentally despise it! They do not want any part of it. Their lawless nature does not want to come under the law or cooperate with any authority figures. So they are in their desires to *"walk after the flesh and the lust of uncleanness."* They take pride in the possessions even though it is all hoarding and takes on the appearance of uncleanness since there is so much clutter and disorder.

- *Presumptuous and self-willed* – 2 Peter 2:10 continues, *"Presumptuous are they, self-willed. They are not afraid to speak evil of dignities."*

It seems they always find fault with someone else. They always feel they could have done whatever job it was better than whoever did it. This superiority complex keeps them from recognizing the deception that is on them. They think the world is against them; that is why they cannot get ahead.

What they need are intercessors who will stand in the gap for them, in Jesus' Name. We must bind the spirit of poverty with all its characteristics on them. Once the light comes on to see the way they are living, especially if they have the light of Jesus in their hearts, they will turn from darkness to light. They will turn from Satan's ways to God's ways and from sin to repentance.

We can have the confidence as it says in Philippians 1:6, *"Being confident of this very thing, that he which hath begun a good work in you will perform it until the day of Jesus Christ."* We are not alone in this progression into the life of God within us. We have the faithful Holy Spirit to perform the work.

1. How many sides are there to deceitfulness of riches?

———————————————————————————

Explain the difference.

———————————————————————————

2. How does the enemy use deceitfulness of riches against the believer?

_____

3. How is grandiose thinking used by the devil?

_____

4. Is it wrong to have riches and possessions?

_____

Explain.

_____

5. How does deceitfulness of riches work on the poverty side?

_____

6. How should the believer pray to become free of deceitfulness of riches?

_____

7. How did the rich young ruler go wrong?

_____

8. What was he established in?

_____

9. What is happening to the person who receives sorrow when they receive a blessing?

_____

10. What should the believer do when they receive a job and another loses that same job?

_____

11. What does deceitfulness of riches do to the believer?

_____

12. Explain how deceitfulness of riches causes the believer to become double-minded?

_____

13. What is the result of not being teachable?

_____

14. Why is it important to keep our priorities in order?

_____

CHAPTER 14

Lusts of Other Things

Psalm 145:16, 19; Galatians 2:20; 2 Peter 1:34; 1 Corinthians 10:14

In the thesaurus, the synonyms for *lust* are "to covet, crave, to have a strong desire." We can have things, but we cannot allow things to have us. As soon as we let material things have us and they get the center of our attention, then our thinking is in *lusts of other things* rather than our relationship with God and desire for God to be first place.

In the dictionary, *lust* means "an intense desire for people, places, and things to be the center of attention, instead of God. It means a desire to gratify the senses, as in bodily appetites." These could be obsessive-compulsive behaviors such as overeating or over-spending, drug addictions of all kinds, or an extreme appetite for sexual gratification.

Using the word *desire* as the definition of lust, we see some positive-thinking *desires* in the Scripture. In Genesis 3:16 we read: "*Unto the woman he said, I will greatly multiply thy sorrow and thy conception; in sorrow thou shalt bring forth children; and thy desire shall be to thy husband, and he shall rule over thee.*"

To have a desire for our husbands is not a bad thing. We want to have a closeness and tenderness in our hearts toward our spouse. Marriage will either be filled with strife and competition, or it will be filled with an equal appreciation and respect for each other.

In 2 Chronicles 1:11–12 we read about Solomon's desire and request from God:

> *"And God said to Solomon, "Because this was in thine heart, and thou hast not asked riches, wealth, or honor, nor the life of thine enemies, neither yet hast asked long life; but hast asked wisdom and knowledge for thyself, that thou mayest judge my people, over whom I have made thee king: Wisdom and knowledge is granted unto thee; and I will give thee riches, and wealth, and honour, such as none of the kings have had that have been before thee, neither shall there any after thee have the like."*

What an unselfish request. God liked it. It was granted to Solomon that he would have the wisdom and knowledge that he desired to rule the people. In addition to all the wisdom and knowledge, he also received wealth, riches, and honor. His enemies were put down. He received everything he requested from God because his heart was in the right place. Solomon is an example to us of right priorities.

Psalm 145:16 says, *"Thou openest Thy hand and satisfies the desire of every living creature."* This is a wonderful picture of God. He is forever generously giving and satisfying the desires of His creation. With God there is no lack or want. Verse 19 says, *"He will fulfill the desire of them that reverence Him. He also will hear their cry and save them."*

Because we have a commitment and have allowed our hearts to be toward God, we do not have to double-check our motives or intents. We must not allow a debate every time we ask God for something. Our requests should be based on the Word, and our decision to serve Him with an honest and pure heart will settle our minds. Our motives are right, and our thoughts are correct. They are established in God. We start by believing and receiving that our motives line up with the Word. We tell our soul that it is established in correct thinking and correct motives. We will not walk in our own counsels. We will consider God in our thinking and in our everyday decisions. We are committed to serve God. Our standard for truth is the Bible. It is to our advantage that men took time to write down the inspired words of God. We can refresh ourselves and continue to receive understanding in God's precepts and principles. Our desires are going to be right desires. Proverbs 11:23 confirms this position: *"The desire of the righteous is only good, but the expectation of the wicked is wrath."*

In the book of Esther, we read about how Haman was consumed by *lusts of other things.* He lusted after a higher position and promotion. At that time, King Ahasuerus promoted Haman and set his seat above the other princes. The king commanded all the king's servants to bow down and reverence him, but Mordecai would not bow down and do reverence to him. Haman noted Mordecai's behavior, and we see the first sign of his offense in Esther 3:5: "And when Haman saw that Mordecai bowed not down, nor did him reverence, then was Haman full of wrath." But Haman changed his mind from laying hands only on Mordecai and decided to destroy Mordecai's people, the Jews, throughout the whole kingdom.

The second time that we read of Haman's offense against Mordecai is in verse 5:9:

> *Then went Haman forth that day joyful and glad of heart: but when Haman saw Mordecai in the king's gate, that he stood not up nor moved for him, he was filled with wrath against Mordecai.*

This was after his private banquet with the king and queen. Haman went home and boasted of all he saw and heard and was proud that he was the only one present. But soon after we read of his rejection statement in verse 13: *"Yet all this availeth me nothing, so long as I see Mordecai the Jew sitting at the King's gate."*

In spite of Haman's anger and schemes to destroy all the Jews of the land, God intervened in a dream to King Ahasuerus and reminded him to read the record books of the Chronicles in the middle of the night. In it was recorded that Mordecai had saved the king's life from treacherous men who tried to kill him. The king asked what reward was given to Mordecai for his act of bravery and learned that nothing had been done for him.

We read in Esther 6:12 another statement of rejection by Haman: *"But Haman hasted to his house, mourning and having his head covered."* This was Haman's response to the reward given to Mordecai; the reward Haman dreamed up for himself. Haman was consumed by *lusts of other things*, especially his position and promotion. In the end, he was hanged on the gallows he was having built for Mordecai.

Lusts are desires we allow to take first place in our soul. All the mind traps are forms of idolatry since we have ourselves on the center stage in our thinking. When we made Jesus our Lord, we gave our lives over to be used of Him. Galatians 2:20 says in the *New International Version*: *"I have been crucified with Christ and I no longer live, but Christ lives in me. The life I live in the body, I live by faith in the Son of God, who loved me and gave himself for me."*

We have been bought and paid for by His blood. God has given us all things now that pertain to life and godliness. Second Peter 1:3–4 (NIV) reads:

> *His divine power has given us everything we need for life and godliness through our knowledge of him who called us by his own glory and goodness. Through these he has given us his very great and precious promises, so that through them you may participate in the divine nature and escape the corruption in the world caused by evil desires.*

We need not yield our minds to idolatry. First Corinthians 10:14 instructs us to flee idolatry: *"Wherefore, my dearly beloved, flee from idolatry."* Every mind trap we have discussed is a picture of our desire to have *self* on the throne. When *self* is center stage, we are engaged in idolatry because it displaces Jesus.

In the *expectation* mind trap, we saw how Naaman expected Elisha to deal with him directly. Because the prophet sent a messenger instead, Naaman became offended and almost missed his healing. We see the *recall* mind trap weaving its web with the children of Israel when they murmured and complained in unbelief in the wilderness. They were expressing their anger and offense at what they did not have instead of being thankful for God's provisions and blessings for what they had and for what He did for them. How many times do we *project* failure and defeat before the actual opportunity comes up? We can all identify with Moses when he was centered on his inability as a speaker. How could he go and speak to Pharaoh? *Assumption* can be deadly when we suppose something to be a fact when it is not. Cain was sidetracked by the mind trap of *comparison* when he centered on Abel's sacrifice instead of pursuing what he knew would please God. He did not have to kill his brother. He could have sacrificed an animal the next time. The Pharisees were so confident in their *intellectualizing* they missed that they were to reason with God and not be stuck in traditions and rituals. Job was held in a no-man's land of despair while his friends *spiritualized* that God must be the reason for his problems. And Adonijah tried to seize the kingdom from his brother Solomon when he *pridefully* proclaimed, "I will be king."

The list goes on and on. I try to check myself when I find I am rehearsing an incident or statement made by myself or another person. This is my clue that I have probably opened up to a mind trap, and I have *self* at the center of my thinking. If there is guilt or condemnation, I repent. If there is disapproval by someone, I forgive. I take back control of my soul by repenting and receiving peace in my mind. This allows my soul to stay in the rest Jesus has provided for me.

If I do not catch the mind trap at this stage, I will find myself in offense. As we will see, there are ways to uncover and recognize our thinking at the offense stage also. Jesus has made the way for us to live in victory. Sometimes we take a detour into defeat, but He always gives us a way of escape.

1. How does lust of other things interfere in our relation with God and His Word?

    _____

2. Why was Solomon so blessed by God?

    _____

3. When will a believer not have to check his/her motives or intent?

    _____

4. Where did Haman go wrong in his relationship with Mordecai?

    _____

5. Why are all the mind traps a form of idolatry?

    _____

6. Why is it wrong to have *self* on the throne?

    _____

7. What is a clue that a believer has opened him or herself up to a mind trap?

    _____

8. Explain how a believer can get out or stop a mind trap and give examples.

    _____

Section III

REACTIONS TO
MIND TRAPS

CHAPTER 1

2 Corinthians 10:4–5; Romans 8:33; Mark 4:7;
James 3:2

The synonyms in the thesaurus for *offend* are "to abuse, to be an affront, to aggravate, alienate, anger, annoy, antagonize, appall, estrange, disgust, exasperate, and outrage." Outrage implies an extreme offense against one's sense of justice. When we become offended, the reaction we have and the attitude we show will be one of anger or one of frustration. We probably will be annoyed, irritated, or even disgusted with a person or a situation.

The synonyms in the thesaurus for *anger* are "displeasure, exasperation, indignation, to be enraged, furious and hostile." And the synonyms for *frustration* are "annoyance, irritation, aggravation, disappointment and a setback."

In the dictionary, *offense* means "to create displeasure and resentment, to anger, to offend, especially feeling hurt, resentful, angry, and frustrated." When we are frustrated, we usually don't see our reaction as being offended, but it is offense. When we know we are frustrated, our question needs to be: "What did I do before I got to this point? I got here. I'm frustrated. Now what in my thinking caused me to reach this place?"

In the *Strong's Concordance*, the word *offends* means "to entrap, trip up, to cause displeasure, to stumble, to entice to sin or apostasy." The purpose of offense is to cause a person to distrust or to leave the one whom he ought to trust. Offense causes one to fall away or to stumble. We have an example of this in John 6:32–69 when Jesus said He was the *Bread of Life*. The Jews murmured against Him, and the disciples said His sayings were hard. In verse 61, Jesus asked them, *"Does this offend you?"* when He realized His disciples were also murmuring. Many stopped following Jesus at this point. They were in the dangerous place of offense. Offense has the potential to be a stumbling block to us. It can cause us to fail and end up in ruin. It may even cause us to fall away from God.

In the *Hebrew Lexicon*, the Old Testament word for *offense* means "to cause a falling or failing of anyone." In Psalm 119:165 it says, *"Great peace have they which love thy law: and nothing shall offend them."* We have the promise of Scripture and the ability not to be offended, but we have to make that decision. We have to decide not to be offended. We have to go through life and say, *"No matter what happens, I refuse to be offended!"* Not harboring any offense against anyone is where we want to be. This is the goal we want to achieve.

Matthew 11:6 says, *"Blessed is he whosoever shall not be offended in me."* Jesus came to be a stumbling block to the doctrines and the teachings of the Pharisees and the Sadducees. He shined a light on their teaching, and it stumbled them. We see throughout the Scriptures that their outlook and statements came from an offended position. Every comment they made had the expectation that Jesus would not expose their high-mindedness and traditions that were contrary to the will of God. They did not appreciate Jesus at all.

In our lives, when we stand up and put forth the Word of God, we cannot be offended if it is not received. Yet it is a normal and natural reaction for us to get angry. We do that whenever our doctrine of thinking or our belief system is not accepted, is ridiculed, or is challenged. We do not like it when others reject our beliefs, but we have to realize that God is used to being rejected, so we had better learn to take it in stride and not take it personally! As His followers, we are also reminded: "Blessed is he whosoever is not offended in me."

Truth is truth! We should not be offended when others reject our Gospel message, nor should we be offended at the messages of truth we get from the Holy Spirit in His transforming work in our lives. There are two areas to watch where offense can come in a strong way and trip us up: when we become offended with unbelievers causing us to lose our testimony and when we resist the work of the Holy Spirit in our lives, thereby delaying our spiritual growth.

In the *New International Version,* Matthew 11:6 reads, *"Blessed is the man who does not fall away on account of me."* In this version, it is saying the man is blessed who will not be offended in Jesus or fall away because of Him. When we are offended with someone, we tend to distance ourselves from them. When we become offended with God, we will move away from Him.

Mark 4:14–21 is the parable of the sower who sows the seed. The seed is the Word. The parable illustrates different kinds of ground and the decision we must make to have a fruitful heart. It says:

> *"The sower sows the word and these are they by the way side, where the word is sown; but when they have heard, Satan comes immediately and takes away the word that was sown in their hearts. And these are they likewise which are sown on stony ground; who, when they have heard the word, immediately receive it with gladness; and have no root in themselves, and so endure but for a time; afterward, when affliction or persecution arises for the word's sake, immediately they are offended. And these are they which are sown among thorns; such as hear the word, and the cares of this world, and the deceitfulness of riches, and the lusts of other things entering in, choke the word, and it becomes unfruitful."*

The enemy comes to steal the Word from us. His weapons are afflictions or pressures, persecutions, the cares of this world, deceitfulness of riches, and the lusts of other things. He brings these things against us to turn our attention away from the Word. When we allow the *cares of this world*, for example, to crowd the Word out, then the Word cannot take root in our lives and it dies.

How many times have we experienced the thrill and gladness in our hearts from understanding God's saving grace and then wanted to share it with someone only to find that it was not received? What happened to us? Most of the time, we allow our minds to take on an expectation that our testimony, as well as our experiences with God, will be accepted. When we are rejected, we try to defend our beliefs and enter into one of the works of the flesh called *strife,* which means trying to get our thoughts, opinions, and beliefs over to another person when they are not open to receive them.

When this happens, we get into an angry contest of words instead of a beautiful sharing around the Word. We walk away not realizing that we have just encountered one of Satan's weapons, and he does this especially well when the seed of the Word is young. He does not want the Word of God to get a root system in us, so he brings persecution for the Word's sake to see if we will get offended.

When Satan suggests to us to share our new revelation with someone, he will also suggest an expectation to go along with it. If we allow the expectation to form in our minds, it will form an image. Remember when we were talking about strongholds? They start with a foundation, and the foundation of the stronghold is the suggestion that forms an image in our minds. The process goes like this: First, we allow a mind trap like expectation into our minds. Second, when it is not fulfilled as we imagined, we get offended. Third, we form a philosophy that locks our thinking in that particular matter. We rationalize, analyze, and go over and over the situation in our minds, which establishes the philosophy. We justify our position within ourselves. The lock in this stronghold is our established philosophy making it impossible for any *new ideas* to become established. Our thinking will become a stronghold. Its purpose is to keep us stuck in an area of our minds. This is why mind traps are such dangerous stumbling blocks to all of us.

According to the *Lexicon*, the word *offended* in Mark 4:17 means "to cause a person to begin to distrust or desert one in whom he ought to trust and obey; to cause to fall away or to stumble." Any one of the mind traps will bring a person to the place of offense. When we become offended, we are on our way to acting angry toward ourselves, a person, a situation, and even toward God. When we become offended with God, we will draw away from Him. Expectation, when not fulfilled, will be followed by offense.

In the example of Cain and Abel, God told them what kind of offering He would receive. Cain assumed God would accept his offering, but when God refused it, he became offended with God and angry with his brother. Satan seized the opportunity of Cain's offense and used it even further by suggesting comparison so he could be doubly offended. It was the mind traps of assumption and comparison that were operating, but offense was also used to bring the end result, which was rejection and depression.

We saw in Luke 7:23 Jesus making the statement, *"Blessed is he who is not offended in me."* When we take offense, we are incensed and we retain anger and bitterness against people. We have all met people who are stuck in offense. They have a chip on their shoulder. They see themselves as innocent victims and are always complaining about their lot in life. Offended people are not winning since they will not play by the rules. They struck out at bat, and now they are sulking on the sidelines. When their turn at bat comes up again, they stick their tongue out and refuse to play. Some struck out years ago and are still sulking on the sidelines, refusing to play.

When Dennis and I were pastors, I fell into offense. People came to visit us on Sunday morning. After the service, they told us how much they enjoyed the sermon and they could not wait to become members of the congregation. But the next Sunday came and went, and they never returned. Other people who had been attending for a while pledged their loyalty and promised to be behind us financially for years to come. We made plans based on their words and found out later that they had left the church. Still other people were in and out of our counseling office for months. We juggled our schedules for them, labored in prayer for them, rejoiced over victory when it came, and then heard that they said we were quacks and heretics.

Of course, not everyone was this way. We did have many loyal members whose word we could trust. If they changed their minds or if their situations changed, they talked to us and our parting was beautiful. But where I ran into trouble was expecting and banking on what people said to us. I let my emotional dependency be on them and not on God. Remember, with expectation comes the hidden need for acceptance and approval. Expectation led me right into offense. I continually saw life through the eyes of offense. I became angry at the way we were treated, and I had no pleasure in serving the people. Everything became a chore. I blew everything out of proportion, and I was sure I was the most hated person in the Saddleback Valley. No matter where I went, I thought someone was sure to know me and hate me. I was consumed with myself, and I went back into a depression that I had been out of for years.

One day as I was getting on the freeway, I asked the Holy Spirit to show me what I was doing wrong. I was ready to hear from Him. I realized the problem had to be with me and not with the people or the circumstances. I was trapped as long as I thought it was someone else's problem for the way I was treated. How many times have we heard people say, "You make me so mad!" That is not true. We first decided to get mad, and then we became mad. It had nothing to do with the people or the circumstances. It was our decision. Whatever happened or was said was independent from our reaction. We need to realize that our reaction to people and circumstances is completely our responsibility.

The Holy Spirit reminded me of my lifelong commitment to Him to not be offended in Him. The important thing I had to realize about the parable in Mark 4 was that in order to be offended, I had to have a stony heart in an area and have no root system in myself. With the Holy Spirit's help, I was able to judge my reactions in that area of my life and get out of my depression.

I will always remember exactly where I was at the time. I was going north on the freeway when the Holy Spirit revealed all this to me. The Holy Spirit's words are forever locked into my consciousness. When I saw that I was offended, I felt bad that an area of my heart was stony and that it had no root system. I thought, *You try to practice the Word and here you are acting like a baby!* So I made a firm decision again to have a good-ground heart and not be offended by people's words or actions. The Holy Spirit also showed me that my expectation was on people, especially on Christians, to live up to their word and my expectations of them, instead of on God. I thought they should keep their word at all times and act like I thought Christians should act. When I saw the expectation thinking, I repented, cast out the words and the images, and received my forgiveness from God. I decided that people mean what they say at the time they say it, but I needed to give them the freedom and the right to change their minds if they wanted to. I stopped trying to get other people's acceptance and approval. I put my dependence back on God for my acceptance and approval, and I have lived by that until this day.

I realized that what people say and the way they act is truth to them at the time. It may be absolutely contrary to the Word, and I may know it is the biggest deception. But you know what? They believe it, and they have the right to believe whatever they want to believe. I cannot say they are wrong or stupid. I just have to accept them and pray for God's will to be done in their lives.

As for the people who did not think highly of our ministry, I simply forgave them. My forgiveness of them did not make what they did right, but it made me right. After all, where would the challenge be if we only forgave those who did nothing wrong? As Jesus said in Matthew 5:43–46:

> *"You have heard that it has been said, Thou shalt love thy neighbor, and hate thine enemy. But I say to you, love your enemies, bless them that curse you, do good to them that hate you, and pray for them that despitefully use you, and persecute you; that you may be the children of your Father which is in heaven: for he makes his sun to rise on the evil and on the good, and sends rain on the just and on the unjust. For if you love them that love you, what reward have you? Do not even the publicans the same?"*

I still use Romans 8:33 today: *"Who shall lay anything to the charge of God's elect? It is God that justifies."* I pray this Scripture this way, "Thank you, Father, You know what is being said and done. You will justify us and also vindicate us. We receive restoration in our relationships with the people, in Jesus' Name." He has been very faithful on our behalf to restore our relationship with many who misinterpreted who we were and what we were teaching when we were pastoring a church.

Becoming offended makes life extremely difficult. Love is the one law we were given by Jesus because it is the principle upon which everything else works. God is love. When we are offended, we cannot flow in love. In fact, we are in direct opposition to it, like swimming upstream, as the saying goes. What if we find ourselves in this position? What can we do about it?

Some people have been collecting offenses like trophies for years. They bring them up and dump them out every time company comes over. They sit in the living room with their after-dinner coffee and tell each story with renewed anger and offense while their guests long for escape. These people are locked in a mind trap and offense. They have formed a philosophy and do not even know it. I am sure we have all come across people like this, but if we are one of them, here is the way to get out of it.

We need to bring out all our trophies one more time and lay them out on the floor. Make a thorough search. The Holy Spirit is very good at helping us with this. Yield to His leading and ask Him in each situation where we went wrong, not where the others involved were wrong. Forgive everyone and then forgive ourselves. We are going to find out that we have been caught in one, or even two or three, of the mind traps. We will see that we formed an image of those people or that situation a long time ago, and we have been locked into our philosophy about them ever since. We must cast out all mind traps, offense, philosophies, rejection, and depression if they are present and receive our forgiveness from the Father. We must repent for our wrong thinking against anyone and receive the peace of God to come into our minds and hearts, in Jesus' Name.

According to 2 Corinthians 10:4–6:

> *For the weapons of our warfare are not carnal, but mighty through God to the pulling down of strongholds: Casting down imaginations, and every high thing that exalteth itself against the knowledge of God and bringing into captivity every thought to the obedience of Christ: And having in a readiness to revenge all disobedience when your obedience is fulfilled.*

These mind traps have exalted themselves above God in our minds. Some of them have been exalted above God for a long time. We need to get our minds back in line with God and ask Him to fill us with His peace and understanding.

A friend of mine shared with me something she had done for years. She had been very critical of herself and would get very offended at herself. She would think negative thoughts all the time like, *How can you be so stupid? How can you think that way? How could you do such a stupid thing?* She was constantly taking offense at herself. She realized if she could not love herself and get rid of negative thinking about herself, she could not love other people. This was such an automatic habit in her life that it became almost commonplace. But the Holy Spirit showed her and said, "How can you love others when you are so down on yourself?" After that, she realized she was not receiving the love toward others from God because she was not giving it to herself first. Seeing this, with the Holy Spirit's help, was good news for her and set her free. This is similar to not forsaking our own mercy that we talked about in another part of this book. We must be good to ourselves and merciful to ourselves first before we can show mercy to others.

When trouble and persecution comes because of the Word, the person without a root system quickly falls away. We cannot take the persecution personally because the persecution is after the Word in us, not after us. This is vital to know for surviving spiritual warfare. The devil plants his words in the mouths of flesh and blood people around us, but those words are really coming from principalities and powers. We think we are dealing with people, but we are really dealing with principalities and powers that are after the Word in us. Our job is to guard the Word. Forgiveness is the fastest way to guard the Word and stop offense.

I have often thought of how Mary, the mother of Jesus, knew some of what was going to happen to Jesus and yet hid those things in her heart. We are to hide new revelations regarding the application of the Word until they have been meditated on and have developed a root system in our hearts. Then it is safe to give them away to others by sharing them, and the devil cannot uproot and destroy the life they have given to us. When we have a revelation established in our hearts, it cannot be taken from us.

In Mark 4:17 it says: *"And have no root in themselves and so endure but for a time, afterward when affliction and persecution arises for the word's sake, immediately they are offended."*

I have seen this many times when people were so enthusiastic about the Word. They got very excited about some revelation they had just had, but that excitement usually set them up for a fall. The seed must be tested by the devil, and it is his goal to get the seed out of us before it develops a root system. Know this and say, "Father, I am thrilled with this knowledge. I am going to hide it now in my heart. I am going to protect it and water it and practice it, but I am not going to go spewing it out to every person around me, especially to those who are not established in the Word."

Even our closest Christian friend who is established in the Word cannot have the same revelation that we have, unless the Holy Spirit gives it to them. They are not going to get the revelation from us, and it is not our job to give them our revelation. It is the Holy Spirit's job. But after we have walked it out and have become established in our revelation and really understand it, then we can start to give it away. Do not share revelations just to get people's reactions because their reactions should not matter to us when we become established in a truth. There is no debate with experience. It is much better to be in the place where our experience has been so sealed in that it does not matter what people think than to share our revelation indiscriminately for a reaction or to get approval from them.

In Acts 24:16 Paul says, *"And herein do I exercise myself, to have always a conscience void of offence toward God, and toward men."* Paul tells us here that he practices not to be offended. He exercises himself not to get offended so that he will get good at doing it. To know that God says it is possible and to find Paul saying, "I'm working on this" is comforting and encouraging to me. Paul said he was striving to do this. The word *strive* has the meaning "to grasp, to seize, or to grab with the hand." He is grasping this and bringing it to himself. He wanted to be blameless without stumbling, so he exercised his conscience to always be void of offense. He is our role model in this exercise.

In James 3:2 it says, *"For in many things we offend all. If any man offend not in word, the same is a perfect man, and able also to bridle his whole body."* We have the ability to do this. We have the ability not to offend with our words. It is a decision we have to make. If a person immediately becomes offended by pressures of life and by persecution, they have a *stony-ground* heart and will have no root system in themselves. They have not taken the time to make the decision to not get offended and to follow through and uphold that decision.

Colossians 2:8 says, *"Be aware lest any man spoil you through philosophy and vain deceit after the traditions of men and after the rudiments of the world and not after Christ."* So the philosophies and vain empty deceits that we take are based on traditions and on the rudiments of the world. The world's principles or ways are contrary to God's ways. Even though we have these *winds of doctrines* all around us by every means of communication, we must not allow these destructive words to find a place in our minds and *spoil* us, as the verse says.

A philosophy can be formed that says, "I am never going to share my heart again. That is the last time I tell them about something that went on in my life!" We know it is just little thoughts, but they are decisions that lock us into a philosophy in an area of our thinking for a long time. And we shut down and cut ourselves off from those people. It is usually based on an anger reaction to a hurt that was caused by the mind trap that we allowed to entrap us.

Philosophies lock us up by what we decide to think, and then rationalizing and analyzing take over. For these two reactions of the mind traps to do their *dirty work*, we had to have sinned against another person or been falsely accused of something.

Rather than forgiving or repenting, we slip into rationalizing. We go over the circumstance in our minds and pick up every thread of excuse for our own behavior and every thread of accusation against the other party. These threads form the yarn of our tapestry of self-justification. Rather than let the *Great Advocate* plead our case, we refuse counsel.

The case never comes to trial; therefore, it is never decided on or finalized. Since it is not put to rest, we have no peace concerning it. We continue to debate it mentally. This restlessness leads us to the next reaction, which is analyzing. Our mind eventually gets tired of constant debating, so we decide the case must be closed. We then act as both judge and jury and mentally preside over the case.

First, we analyze the prosecutor's story, then the side of the defense. From all these facts, we make our judgment and pass sentence. We either condemn ourselves or the other party, but we have refused to repent and accept God's forgiveness for either our own sin or for the other person's actions. Regardless of our decision or the outcome, we are now well entrenched in sin.

The end result the devil is after is either physical suicide, marital suicide, job suicide, or relationship suicide. These all result in the death of something in the end, and that loss opens us up to deep grief and depression.

Sometimes the verdict goes against the other party, but this can be equally harmful. A friend of mine was working for a company that was very poorly run and that caused her much frustration. She did her job well, but she spoke to the other employees about the management problems she encountered within the company. She was especially frustrated by the actions of the owner of the company and told others about his mistakes.

She knew gossiping was wrong, and her heart condemned her of this sin. But rather than repent, she began to rationalize her behavior. She told herself that it was entirely the boss's fault. He was not trustworthy, and she felt she had to warn the other employees of the situation so they could look for other jobs before the business collapsed or they were laid off. Besides, she felt that she was being treated unfairly and had to let off steam. Of course, this line of thinking brought her no peace, so the case had to be mentally tried and closed.

After analyzing both sides carefully, the scales tipped in her favor and she condemned her boss. When the business prospered, it rankled her sense of justice yet it was her job to help it to prosper. Finally, she had to quit, but she took her bitterness with her and entered into another almost identical situation. It all happened because of what she allowed to go on in her thinking. This could have gone on indefinitely affecting her in every business position she took, but thank God, He revealed the cycle to her. She repented, forgave herself and her former bosses, and was set free from repeating this behavior pattern over again.

If we find ourselves mulling over a situation, a conversation, or an accusation, recognize that rationalizing and analyzing are behind the debate in our minds. As we run these condemning thoughts back and forth mentally realize that whatever verdict we decide on will become our trap. It will entrap us since these are images that are exalting themselves against the knowledge of God. It is our job to cast these images down in Jesus' Name! It is an important principle to recognize that we do not always have to be right to get our point across. *Cleaning up* what we have allowed to *dirty up* our minds by repenting and receiving our forgiveness or forgiving someone else's words and actions will start us back on the road to recovery. If we do this, we will be able to enter into the rest that Jesus has given us for our minds.

The walls are built onto a foundation, and they started with an image that we allowed into our minds with a mind trap. When we get offended, we have already been taken captive by a mind trap and we build a wall called offense. Another wall will be rejection and another will be depression, and it all will be locked up with a philosophy that is made after much rationalizing and analyzing has been done. A philosophy is no more than a decision that says, *"This is the way it is! No matter what anybody else says, this is the way I'm thinking about this. I've got my mind made up, and I'm not going to budge!"* We can be locked into a philosophy for moments, hours, days, weeks, months, years, or for a whole lifetime! It is all up to us. It is our decision.

Thank God we have Jesus inside of us, and as we keep yielding to the Holy Spirit, things are continually coming to the light. It is His ministry to show us the unrighteousness in our thinking. All of us were trapped in the world's unrighteous system of thinking. There is unrighteousness that is deeply seated within our souls, and it is the Holy Spirit's ministry to bring it to the light. As we read the Word of God and put it into our hearts, it will renew our minds. The Holy Spirit will continue to bring to us all the characteristics of Jesus, who is the Word. As the *Truth,* He will set us free from our mind traps. With His help, we can break down all the walls that the mind traps have built. He will enlighten us so we can repent and change our minds and any of the philosophies that we have made. We have an *Advocate*, a *Helper*, and the *Spirit of Truth* who lives inside of us. Jesus has already placed the deliverance from these traps in our hearts. All we have to do is grab hold of it. He said, "I will never leave you nor forsake you." He will never leave us alone to figure these things out for ourselves. He is always with us, especially in our time of need.

1. What is the purpose of offense against a believer?

   _____

2. Why is offense so dangerous to a believer's walk?

   _____

3. How do we keep from being offended in our Christian life?

   _____

4. What is wrong with the statement, "You make me so mad?"

    _____

5. How do people get from right thinking into offense?

    _____

    What is the catalyst or cause?

    _____

6. What is the biggest clue we have when we find ourselves in offense?

    _____

7. Once we find ourselves in offense, how do we break the offense and walk in love?

    _____

8. What is the purpose of persecution against a believer?

    _____

9. What is the best tool a Christian has to fight persecution?

    _____

10. Based on Mark 4:7, how do we protect ourselves from being offended?

    _____

11. What is the best way to keep and protect a new revelation?

   _____

12. Using James 3:2, explain how can we keep from being offended.

   _____

13. Why is it extremely important to recognize and eliminate a philosophy in our minds?

   _____

14. How do we break a recognized or revealed philosophy formed against another individual?

   _____

15. How does rationalizing and analyzing work against us?

   _____

16. How can rationalizing and analyzing be broken?

   _____

17. Explain the transition that takes place in our minds after becoming offended?

   _____

18. Whose ministry is it to protect us from falling into philosophy?

_____

What is our part?

_____

CHAPTER 2

Rejection/Depression

Romans 8:1–2; John 10:10; Isaiah 53:4; Proverbs 13:12

In the thesaurus the synonyms for *reject* are "cast away, cast down, despise, turn from, and disallow." For the word *rejection* the synonyms are "condemnation, disapproval, or forsaking;" and for *depression* they are "discouragement, despair, despondency, to be melancholy, and to have sorrow."

In the dictionary, *rejection* is defined as "to discard or throw out as worthless, useless or substandard." If you have ever experienced rejection, then you know this is exactly how a person thinks of themselves—substandard, worthless, and useless. We also can think we are cast out, thrown away, or discarded. We have taken as truth what has been said or the actions of others that we have allowed to affect us. When we get into *depression*, it is characterized by *failure, inadequacy, discouragement, and hopelessness.*

Once every month in my own life, I got to the place where I wanted to die. I regularly found myself in depression. The cause of my depression, at the time, was the common symptoms of premenstrual syndrome or PMS. Every month, I became moody and intolerant. I hated myself and everyone around me, especially those who were the nearest and dearest to me. I sank into an emotionally hopeless state. I had experienced the effects of depression for years. When this depressive-thinking state appeared, I did not realize what was happening to me for many months. To counter this, I chose not to trust my thinking and judged my words beforehand to see if there was love in them. With God's grace, I have been able to overcome this pattern of thinking. I found the way to have victory over it and experience total peace with myself.

When rejection came at me, it was always followed by depression. Since rejection brings depression, we can avoid it with right thinking. There is a rightful thinking we can choose to have when rejection comes, and it will counteract its effects. When rejection hits, there are places in Scripture we need to go immediately. If we read and meditate on these verses when we are faced with rejection, they will hold our minds and will give us the ability to deal with our emotions. There is right thinking and wrong thinking in every situation, and the choice is up to us. In the majority of the mind traps, there is a right way of thinking that will give us victory over it and a wrong way of thinking that will take us under into depression. Rejection comes to all of us, and we have to be ready for it. If we are ready, we will not go all the way down into depression.

2 Corinthians 10:6 tells us to have a readiness to revenge the thoughts or imaginations that come to us that are disobedient to Christ and to His Word. We have to recognize the thoughts that contain rejection and depression in them and say no to them. We have to catch the thoughts that are mind traps and say, "This is not my thought!" or "I will not own this thinking as my thinking!"

In secular psychology, these thought patterns are called negative self-talk. Many self-improvement programs address these destructive thought patterns and urge people to eliminate them from their habits of thinking. Negative self-talk has the potential to take us deeper into hopelessness and depression. Wrong thinking and negative self-talk are one and the same thing.

The promises in Psalm 9:10 are: *"And they that know thy name will put their trust in thee: for thou, Lord, hast not forsaken them that seek thee."* Whatever negative or unpleasant circumstance comes into our lives, we have to be in the place in our thinking of trusting God since He said He will never leave us nor forsake us. God will go through it with us, uplift us, and help us to overcome the situation. People will forsake us, but God will never forsake us. It does not matter how close the person is to us, they will forsake us sooner or later in some manner. It can be our spouse, our children, our mother, our father, or another close relative or friend. They will all forsake us at some point in time. It is not that they even intend to, but they are going to center on themselves before they center on us, and in that process, they will forsake us.

Psalm 22:24 says, *"For he has not despised my cries of deep despair; he has not turned and walked away when I cried to him, he turned and came."* Psalm 34:5 says, *"Others too were radiant at what he did for them. Theirs was no down cast look of rejection."* God's promise to us when we walk with Him in His Scriptures is that there will be no downcast look on our face. When we are walking in hurt and rejection, we will look downcast; we will be looking at the floor. But Psalm 34 says they had a radiance about them because of what He did for them. They knew who their source of supply was. To always know that God is on our side has a very stabilizing effect on our rampant thoughts in times of trial.

When rejection comes at us, we can go to Romans 8:1: *"There is therefore now no condemnation to them which are in Christ Jesus, who walk not after the flesh, but after the Spirit."*

The word *condemnation* also means rejection. So this verse could be reworded as such: There is therefore now no rejection to them which are in Christ Jesus.

The whole point in these promises from Scripture is that in order to maintain ourselves, we must stay in the light. This means we must stay in the Word. Maintaining ourselves means to stay in the light and stay in the Word as much as we can. The Word helps us keep our thought-life under God's control. Romans 8:31 says, *"If God be for us, who can be against us."* In Romans 8:33 we read, *"Who shall lay anything to the charge of God's elect? It is God that justifies."* He is our defense attorney! Psalm 37:25 promises: *"I have been young, and now am old; yet have I not seen the righteous forsaken, nor his seed begging bread."*

Another thing to remember is that according to Scripture, we are blessed when we have condemnation coming at us and we have not sinned. It is considered a blessing in Scripture when we have not done anything wrong and are being wrongly condemned. First Peter 2:20 says:

> *"For what glory is it if, when you are buffeted for your faults, you shall take it patiently? But if, when you do well, and suffer for it, you take it patiently, this is acceptable with God."*

When we have pressures coming at us or we are wrongly persecuted and take it patiently, that is acceptable to God. If we sustain losses while doing good for others and we take it patiently, God is pleased. We must see the source of these pressures and persecutions. John 10:10 tells us: *"The thief cometh not, but for to* steal, *and to* kill, *and to* destroy: *I am come that they might have life, and that they might have it more abundantly."*

The losses, pressures, and persecutions come from the devil; and life abundant comes from God. Jesus has come to give us life and that more abundantly. We must know the source for these things in our lives. When we stand against the pressures brought on by the devil and people who are the devil's advocates to annihilate us, we actually will build character and endurance.

In Scripture, we have the picture of God the Father who was rejected by His people time and time again. One such example is in 1 Samuel 12:10:

> *And they cried unto the Lord and said we have sinned, because we have forsaken the Lord. We have served Baalim and Ashtaroth. But now deliver us out of the hand of our enemies and we will serve thee.*

This is a picture that we see over and over again on how the people of Israel rejected God. God wanted to lead and rule His People Himself, but they wanted a king to rule over them instead. They rejected God's authority over their lives and wanted to be ruled by human authority.

In addition to this picture in Samuel of God the Father, we see a picture of Jesus Christ, the Son of God, who took upon Himself all our sins and all the judgment that was against us. For His sacrificial act, He was *rejected of men* and is still being *rejected of men* today. When rejection comes to us, it helps to look at God the Father's experience with the nation of Israel and Christ the Son's experience when His own people rejected Him. It helps us to know that our Father and our Lord both experienced rejection and didn't lose faith.

David and others who have gone before us in Scripture also experienced rejection. They all had to suffer rejection from men, and we do not come even close to anything they experienced, especially the rejection that the Father and the Son experienced. We can go to them and get comfort for the rejection in our lives, and we can thank Jesus for what He has done. He is our substitute. He took our rejection from men and bore it on the cross for us. We need to see that He already suffered for us. This is why we do not have to fall into rejection and suffer since it has been borne and defeated. He gave us a way out.

I have often read Isaiah 53:4 to comfort myself. It says, *"Surely he hath borne our grief and carried our sorrows: yet we did esteem him stricken, smitten of God, and afflicted."* Grief and sorrows refer to both physical and emotional sickness and disease. When my spirit is hurting because I have allowed the hurt of rejection to get all the way into my spirit, I am experiencing sorrow and broken-heartedness.

I remember driving on the freeway and crying out to God for help and that Scripture in Isaiah came to my mind. When I realized that He already bore my grief and sorrows on the cross, the burden of them lifted right off and left me. They seemed to pass out of the top of my head and right through the roof of my car. They were gone from me, and I said, "Thank You, Lord!" in relief.

In Luke 6:22 it says:

> *"Blessed are ye, when men shall hate you, and when they shall separate you from their company, and shall reproach you, and cast out your name as evil, for the Son of Man's sake."*

These words from the Sermon on the Mount can help us remember that when these things come, God wants us to be prepared. If we see from God's perspective that we are blessed when men hate us and reject us, we will be able to have the right attitude during persecution and rejection. We will be able to find comfort in this verse and endure persecution because of our stand.

We hear about Christians all over the world who are persecuted for their religious beliefs. They are paying the ultimate price today for their stand. They are giving their lives. But we are also persecuted here at home when our children mock us or laugh at us. That is also a form of persecution and rejection. We are to recognize that things will happen to us, and we should not be surprised or devastated by them when they do. Many times persecution and rejection come from our nearest and dearest relationships, from those who can hurt us the most when we least expect it.

To our natural minds, it is foolishness to suffer rejection for the Gospel's sake. But we must remember that Jesus told us that as they hated Him, the world would hate us too. He went before us, and He was able to endure. Since we have Him inside of us, dwelling in us, we can depend on His ability to endure through these times of rejection. His life in us can even enable us to pray for the very people who reject us and hurt us. We must not retain it against them. We need to receive ourselves justified. Do not stay on the defensive. We need to get back on the offensive and say, "I thank You, Father, I am justified." We are already justified. When rejection comes, we can comfort ourselves with the Word of God. Yes, this helps when things are happening to us, but we also need to take action by getting back on the offensive!

This is when we have to say, "Thank You, Father. Who can charge anything against the elect of God? It is God who justifies." We quote Scriptures aloud to hold our minds and emotions in check. We can go back on the offensive by remembering what the Word says about the thief who has stolen from us. "If you've taken from me, Satan, you must pay me back sevenfold, in Jesus' Name." Keep Proverbs 6:30–31 in mind, which says when the thief is found *"he must repay sevenfold."*

The Bible says we are to walk in the love of God and be kind and gentle to one another. We are not to be puffed up and seek our own way, and yet we do these things daily. Our behavior looks hopeless at times, but we can endure and bear all things if we know we have the One in us who can do all these things. We can believe in ourselves to change, and we can have hope for our future because we have the One in us who can walk in the love of God. He can be kind and gentle to others. His life is not puffed up, and He does not seek His own way. When we live our lives with His life, we can do all the things Scripture says to do. We cannot do it in our own flesh and with our human willpower, but we can do it with His life and by using His Word.

When the Bible says to bear all things and endure all things, it does not mean that we are to go along with somebody when they do something that is wrong. If they steal or cheat or lie, we do not have to go along with their actions. This is where the persecution and rejection usually occurs because they will mock us for being a prude or for being too modest when we do not agree with what they are doing. They will tease us by calling us puritans, goody two-shoes, or worse!

Do not associate with a crowd that does evil things because it reflects on us. We are to not put ourselves in a condoning or compromising position where we become part of the wrongful conduct of ·the whole group. "Flee all appearance of evil." This is where we have to draw the line. When we draw the line, light speaks and darkness hates it! The people in the dark think it is foolish to be honest and good. This is when persecution and rejection will come at us. Do not take it personally because the persecution is trying to steal the Word of God from us. It is better to be prepared and expect their persecution and rejection than to be surprised and devastated by it. Do not be a people pleaser because then we are our peer group's puppet. They will be able to control us. We can expect it, but we do not have to take it! We do not have to go all the way into rejection. When their words or actions hurt, this is when we are in rejection. Choose not to take this thinking.

Persecution is a mind trap, and it will take us on a mind trip! If we allow it to work in our minds and if we give it place, we are going to get offended at what is happening to us and at our so-called prude position. We are going to get offended at God for His ways because we will ask ourselves, "Why do I have to take this hard road? Why did You call me to this? Why do I have to be hated? I don't want to be hated by people!" So we get mad at God! Then we get mad at the people who bring the persecution and rejection into our lives. We get mad at everybody! We can even get mad at the Bible study leader who taught us that God considers it a blessing to be persecuted for doing good.

To save ourselves from going down the same road over and over again and taking the persecution-rejection mind trap trip, we have to make the decision to believe that God meets all our needs according to His riches in glory by Christ Jesus. This means from now until the day of Christ Jesus! Until that day, we have to have the mind-set that our needs are going to be met even though there will be conflicts and challenges because of our stand.

Our stand is either going to be for God or against God. We cannot serve two masters. We will either serve one or the other; there is no riding the fence! People try to ride the fence, but it really does not work. We have to settle our position within ourselves. We have to come to the place where we realize that we are consecrated and dedicated to God for our whole lifetime. We cannot fear people and what they think and say about us. The things that are happening to us are momentary for our life on earth is temporal. We are only going to be here for a little while, but we are going to be in heaven with God for eternity. We must think these things through, make our decisions, and keep it set in our minds (Galatians 2:20).

Our children, no matter what their age, will put pressure on us. They want us to be a certain way and to think and act their way. In my experience, because we had a blended family, when they started talking against my husband, I had to say, "You will not talk against my husband that way!" To our children I had to say, "You will not speak about your father with that tone of voice in my presence! I have committed my whole lifetime to him, and you are here in our house for only a short time!" We must let them know where we draw our boundaries. We have to let them know what we will and what we will not tolerate! We must do that with our children, and we even have to do that with our spouse. We have to do that with our family and with our friends. We have to do that with our coworkers and with employers or employees.

My friend recently started substitute teaching. She was sent to a different school every day, but the same thing happened everywhere she went. The classrooms were *out of control* until she decided to draw her boundary line and tell the students right from the start what she expected of them. She still had trouble with authority figures because her father physically abused her as a child. She had a hard time being strict and firm because she confused it with being abusive and threatening. After she suffered with chaos and anarchy for a few weeks, she realized there had to be some consequences for the students' out of control behavior. She now tells them that it is up to them who gets their name on the board and loses their recess time. If their behavior is unacceptable after recess, they lose the next day's recess. She has more peace and control now in every classroom she teaches.

In both Matthew 21:42 and Mark 12:10, Scripture says, *"The stone the builders rejected has become the head of the corner."* The head of the corner is the *chief cornerstone* in another translation. The cornerstone in architecture is the stone that holds the building up. It is crucial to the strength of the whole structure. Jesus is our cornerstone, and He was rejected.

In 1 Peter 2:7 we read: *"Unto you therefore which believe, he is precious: but unto them which be disobedient, the stone which the builders disallowed, the same is made the head of the corner."*

Jesus was lifted up in spite of everyone's opinion of Him. He was rejected of men, but He was still lifted up to a place of glory back to the Father, and He lifted us all up with Him. That is our position as believers—high and lifted up with Him.

There are other Scriptures that teach us what to do when our hearts become disquieted or our minds give us pictures of depression. Matthew talks about what we are promised when we withdraw ourselves from family or friends who bring us down spiritually or emotionally. In Matthew 19:29 we read:

> *"And every one that hath forsaken houses, or breth-ren, or sisters, or father, or mother, or wife, or chil-dren, or lands, for my name's sake, shall receive a hundredfold and shall inherit everlasting life."*

Sometimes it is profitable for us to withdraw ourselves and keep a guard on what we share with people who may trample over the truth that we are learning. This applies especially to those who are young in the Word of God. Those who are new in the Lord may want to share with everyone in their exuberance, but we must watch over the Word in our hearts and not put it out before swine, as it says in Matthew 7:6: *"Give not that which is holy unto the dogs, neither cast ye your pearls before swine, lest they trample them under their feet, and turn again and rend you."*

Not only will our precious spiritual insights or pearls be destroyed, but we ourselves will suffer violence and hurt. It is up to us to protect the *words of life* that God has given us. These are our *pearls.* If we do not consider whom we are sharing with, they may be yielding to *swine* who will use their mouths to turn and trample our words and tear our hearts.

Rejection is the type of hurt we experience with offense or on the heels of offense. First we become offended, and then we fall into rejection. It is the attitude of rejection that we take on, and it comes after a real or imaginary loss. If we go back to some of our examples in the mind trap section, we will see rejection at work.

Rejection was the attitude taken by the prodigal son's brother in Luke 15:29: *"Yet thou never gavest me a kid, that I might make merry with my friends."* He saw that their father sacrificed a kid goat and had a party when the prodigal son came back home. The brother, who stayed home the whole time, felt rejected because he did everything right but was never rewarded with a sacrificed kid goat. He had access to his inheritance at the same time as the younger son but never put claim to anything. It sounds like he assumed he could not make merry with his friends and became offended with his brother and Father. We can hear the rejection in the words: "You never gave me a party. You never gave me anything, and I stayed here and worked for you without complaining all these years. You gave it to him, and he did not deserve it. I never ran off like he did. I never demanded or wasted my inheritance like he did. And this is how I get treated? It's not fair!"

Rejection is also seen working in Cain in Genesis 4:3–5, and it sounds like this: *"And Cain was very wroth,"* which is offense, *"and his countenance fell,"* which is rejection because his sacrifice was not received by God. It was not received because it was not given with the right attitude of heart and in obedience to the sacrifice God said to give Him.

Miriam, in Numbers 12:2, said, *"Has the Lord indeed spoken only by Moses?"* Miriam and Aaron rose up against their brother Moses. They were offended and angry with him. Here is Miriam's rejection statement: *"Has He not spoken also by us?"* She was right. God did also speak through the two of them, but when God chose their brother Moses to be the spokesman, Miriam and Aaron felt rejected.

Rejection is also seen in the rich young ruler when Jesus told him to sell all he had and give it to the poor. Jesus meant that he would then have treasure in heaven, but we read his response in Luke 18:23: *"And when he heard this, he was very sorrowful for he was very rich."* Jesus said, *"Come, follow me."* He offered the rich young ruler an apostleship position and everything the disciples had and were inheriting, but his treasure was his earthly riches. He did not want to give up his material possessions to gain spiritual ones. He had no desire to store up for himself any spiritual treasures in heaven.

When we take the thinking of rejection, we go into rejection. When a person is in rejection, their words always sound like they are overwhelmed by their own inadequacy, self-pity, or sorrow accompanied by an attitude of self-incrimination, to name just a few. Being in a state of rejection is serious since it opens our minds to the vice grip of depression. Rejection leads us into depression, and depression manifests itself through discouragement, hopelessness, failure, defeat, morbidity, suicide, and death. When we are experiencing any of these, we have been taken over by the devices of the devil.

John 10:10 tells us that *"The thief comes not but to steal, kill, and destroy."* If the devil can steal us away from the Word, he can kill our hopes. Without hope, our vision is gone and our success in life in any area is destroyed. The devil also wants to wreak havoc with our emotions. If we go with the devil's program, it will not be well with our soul. There is no rest for our emotions with him. The devil is a hard taskmaster. It is our job to not let the devil take our attention off the Word by allowing mind traps to exalt themselves above the knowledge of God.

In 1 Kings 18 we read how Elijah defeated all the prophets of Baal on Mount Carmel and turned the hearts of the people back to the Lord. After this amazing miracle, Elijah received a message from Queen Jezebel threatening his life for what he had done. Then a very surprising thing happened to a man who had just called fire down from heaven, destroyed 450 evil prophets of Baal, and began and ended a three-and-a-half-year drought with a single spoken command. He ran for his life! He let Jezebel intimidate him. He crumbled under her threat. Why would a prophet of God, who was moving in the power of God to such a degree, be afraid of one evil woman? In 1 Kings 19:10, we see what happened:

> *"And he said, I have been very jealous for the Lord God of hosts: for the children of Israel have forsaken thy covenant, thrown down thine altars, and slain thy prophets with the sword; and I, even I only, am left; and they seek my life, to take it away."*

Elijah fell into the mind trap of assumption. He assumed Jezebel was able to kill him, and he assumed that he was the only Godly man left in all Israel. He was also offended with God that they should be seeking to kill him. By taking this blaming attitude toward God, he turned away from Him and felt isolated and rejected. We see him hiding in caves and fearing for his life, immersed in self-pity, which is rejection. In verse 10, he tells God that he alone has been obedient, done everything right, and been zealous. He thought everyone else had sinned and turned their backs on God. We can also see depression at work in verse 4: *"And he requested for himself that he might die; and said, It is enough; now, O Lord, take away my life; for I am not better than my fathers."*

People in depression will frequently think thoughts and speak words like, "If only I were dead," or "I just want to die." The hopelessness that is experienced in depression is responsible for this death wish. This is not suicide speaking, this is death speaking. With all the images of defeat, hopelessness, and death running through the mind, the body will experience lethargy, listlessness, and paralyzing fatigue.

These mind traps can take us on an emotional roller-coaster ride if we fall into them. We can experience all these immobilizing emotions while we are caught up in them. But thank God we can get out of all these mind traps as soon as we decide and choose to live by the Word of God. We need to exercise ourselves to recognize Satan's mind traps and not accept them.

It is the same with depression. All it takes is a decision to go back to what we believed from the Word. We need the Word to hold our minds and emotions in check. Go back to where our confidence was. Go back to what we believed and set our hope again on the Word. If we do this, we will come out of depression. It says, *"Hope deferred makes the heart sick."* What is one of the most common symptoms of depression? It is hopelessness. We have to have a healthy amount of hope to stay out of depression. When we lose our hope, our faith will not work either. Hope is like the underwear to faith. We have to have it. It is foundational!

In John 14:15 Jesus said, *"If you love me, keep my commandments."* We must first have love, which is an awareness. The love that we possess within ourselves is the love that God has put there. If we know His precepts and His principles and who He is, we will walk in the love of God. When we come to realize His character and what He has done for us, we will experience the love of God within us. And when we see who He made us to be, we can have hope based on God's character and God's love.

The Bible says, *"God so loved the world that He gave His only begotten son."* He loved us first before we even knew Him. If we realize this is God's principle, it will maintain our hope.

Proverbs 13:12 says, *"Hope deferred maketh the heart sick: but when the desire cometh, it is a tree of life."* It is a tree of life to us when we see the fulfillment of our dream or a manifestation of our hope. God is the one who puts desires in our hearts to fulfill them. Take hold of those desires, based on the love of God, and take hold of who He is and what He promised in His Word. This is how we can keep the hope there in our hearts and in our minds. Do not allow it to be taken away from us by depression or by any of the mind traps. If we stay out of all these mind traps that we have been talking about, we will stay out of depression because all the mind traps lead into depression.

Some people get stuck in depression for years. When we stay out of depression, our hope can easily be maintained. Faith will then work for us because it will be a springboard for our hope. Our goal will be to speak, in line with the Word of God, those words we have received from God. With the hope that is in our hearts and the faith-filled words that come out of our mouths, we will experience abundant life.

When we are speaking the Word of God twenty-four hours a day, our life will become an abundant life for us because we will be receiving it from God. It is not our burden to maintain ourselves. It is God's job to maintain us, and He does it with His Word and with the help of the Holy Spirit. He is continuing to move us forward, and we are possessing the land that He has given us to possess. He will eventually bring us to the place where we will be strong enough to stand and occupy the land.

Now for the end of Elijah's story. Even though Elijah was in depression, God sought him out and got him out of it. How did Elijah get out of depression? He listened to the still small voice of God and followed God's instructions for his life and for the people God wanted him to protect.

This is so important. I saw this again a couple of weeks ago. I realized the devil had killed my vision. Whenever I feel hopelessness, heaviness, or depression, I ask myself, "Where is my hope?" Because as soon as I realize my goal has been moved and the Word has been stolen from me, I get out of depression in a flash! We do not even have to speak to depression. All we have to do is say, "Hey, where's my goal, Father? I receive my goal back." Then we are out of depression. It is that fast and that easy! It all comes with awareness of the effects of the mind traps.

Much of what we experience seems so heavy but with a quick mental assessment and awareness, we can confound the enemy, reverse our situation, and we are out of it! The battle is in our minds, and we give it as much importance as we decide to give it. It is up to us. The Bible says, *"Resist the devil and he will flee."* We really can resist the devilish thoughts and mind traps, and they will flee. Many times we make such a big deal out of the attacks and negative experiences. But as soon as we get back on the Word, we are out of the rejection and depression. It cannot have a hold on us except the hold we give it.

1. How can we avoid rejection? What can we do to counteract its effects? How can we maintain a rightful thought-life?

   _____

2. What is a good way to deal with grief and sorrow?

   _____

3. When we are persecuted and rejected, what is our best weapon and position?

   _____

4. What does the Bible tell us to do when we catch a thief?

    _____

5. How do we best deal with those who are close to us?

    _____

6. What principle can we learn from Matthew 7:6?

    _____

7. Explain the connection between rejection and offense.

    _____

8. What does rejection sound like?

    _____

9. Where does rejection lead to?

    _____

10. In John 10:10, what is the devil after in us?

    _____

11. What is the lesson to be learned from Elijah in 1 Kings 19:10?

    _____

12. What are the thoughts and words depression speaks?

    _____

13. How do we get out of depression?

   _____

14. Explain the relationship between depression, hope, and faith.

   _____

15. What does the abundant life sound like?

   _____

16. How did Elijah get out of depression?

   _____

17. Can we expect this to work for us?

   _____

SECTION IV

RECOVERY FROM
MIND TRAPS

CHAPTER 1

Restoration and Maintenance

3 John 2; James 1:21;
Romans 12:1–3; 2 Corinthians 10:4–5

Now that we have looked at fourteen mind traps that all lead to offense, rejection, and depression, the question is, how do we avoid falling into them? Let us look at the maintenance plan we can follow to keep us from these mind traps and established in the right kind of thinking.

In the thesaurus, the synonyms for *restoration* are "an atonement, compensation, restitution, satisfaction, redemption, amends and indemnity." The word *maintaining* means, "affirm, claim, continue, possess, profess, protect and sustain." In the dictionary, *restoration* is "a putting or bringing back into a former or normal or unimpaired state or condition."

Restoration means to restore the control of the mind to the spirit man. Where the devil has used a part of our thinking, we are bringing back our thoughts to their former unimpaired state. When we are in our spirit, we are in our rightful thinking. We are unimpaired. As soon as we take on wrong thinking, we are impaired from seeing truth. The longer our thinking is distorted by a suggestion spoken to our minds, the more our will is taken from us. It is a form of deception that temporarily deceives us. The control of our minds needs to be by our spirit-man, not by the devil.

Since the mind is a part of the soul of man, it should not be generating of itself because it will center on its own needs. Our soul is like a computer with a memory bank with access to the knowledge of our whole lifetime. It is where different information has been stored. If it is used in the correct way, we can recall the decisions we have made that are truth for us. We can tap into all the resources that we have gained and have been given by the Holy Spirit. I have found that my soul is not to be centered on *self* or taking on some pattern of thinking from the outside. This type of activity keeps my soul busy, and my spirit locked up. Instead, my spirit-man should be flowing freely through my soul and able to express what is there through my mouth. This is the proper functioning of my mind. The source for my mind should be my spirit and not the devil's suggestions. This is the way I can maintain myself and enjoy the rest in my soul that Jesus has bought for me.

Maintaining is "to keep or hold a place or position against attack." We are to defend our position in Christ. When we are main-taining ourselves, we will be experiencing the place that God has made for us. We will be experiencing rest in our souls. God wants our souls to be at rest and under the authority of our spirits. When our spirit-man is generating or *turned on* and functioning to the best of our ability, then we are fulfilling the will of God.

The soul is to be the vehicle of the spirit. It includes the mind using the intellect, will, and emotions. We have our will as our decid-ing place. We constantly say to ourselves, "I'm going to think this way," or "I'm going to think that way." We make decisions all day long; this is our will functioning. At the same time, our intellect is our storage unit. If we put garbage in, we will get garbage out! What God wants is for us to put good things in so that we can get good things out—things that are in line with our spirit-man.

There are many fields of knowledge in the world that are worth studying. God is not against our having knowledge or using our intellect. He gave both of them to man. He wants our spirit filled with His Word and thereby be the source of our soul's operation, and He wants our souls to express what is in our spirits.

For instance, if we study microbiology before going into the field of nursing, it will give us information of the origins of various diseases and their treatments. It can be helpful for our career, and it is not evil for us to study the various sciences. It can be very valuable to us in helping others. We can have an art major and study art history from the beginning of time to the present. There is nothing wrong with studying art. It is a valid body of knowledge. We have to see what the calling is on a person's life and how they are going to minister, and then we will see that there is knowledge in the world that is valid for them. Some Christians become so spiritually goofy, they think everything is worldly and evil.

Another part of our soul is our emotions. Our emotions can either help us or harm us. Emotions include our feelings, our understanding, and our compassion for people. We want these abilities to be generating from our spirits where the love of God is and coming through our souls. If we are operating out of our soulish flesh, we will be too emotional. We may even indulge our undisciplined emotions on ourselves and have frequent pity parties. However, when our emotions are governed by our spirits, they will be healthier for us and for those around us.

On the other hand, our soul can pick up emotions along the way that are in line with our spirit-man so that we are not unfeeling, uncaring individuals. We do not want to look like a piece of stone. People relate better to us when they know we understand them, and we have been through the same circumstances they are going through. Neither of these emotional extremes is healthy: the overly dripping-with-honey emotions and the cold deep freeze of no emotions. Only the emotions tempered by our human spirits that is in contact with the Holy Spirit can show the genuine love of God to people.

Then we have our attitudes. Attitudes are spiritual forces. God has emotions. God has a will, and God definitely has a mind. In Him is all wisdom and knowledge and understanding to be found. He has all kinds of attitudes that we are to walk in. The ninefold fruit of the Spirit listed in Galatians 5 are all attitudes: love, joy, peace, long-suffering or patience, gentleness, goodness, faith or faithfulness, meekness, and self-control. These are all attitudes that come out of our spirits and travel through our souls. When we allow them to be developed in our souls, they will become established. Our emotional attitudes become our habits of behavior, and they will determine the way we are. When we practice attitudes, either good ones or bad ones, we give our wills over to them and they become established in our lives.

Since most of us have taken our knowledge from the world system of thinking before we became new creatures in Christ, we have many attitudes and habits that are contrary to God's attitudes. We must know about, deal with, keep bound, and uproot completely those attitudes that are working against us. We need to go through a process of recognizing them and replacing them with the attitudes of God. This is the program of transformation that we are all in. This is what renewing our minds is all about.

We need to make a decision to take on the mind of Christ. We need to keep our minds on the things that are above. We need to ask ourselves some questions: What is the love of God? How can we show His love to those around us in our lives? What did we see Jesus do in the gospels? Ask ourselves for whatever we are going through, "What would be His attitude in this case?" We can explore these questions and answer them for ourselves. And then we need to identify and take on God's attitudes in our circumstances. The easiest way to become like someone is to hang out with them. In the same way, God's habits of thinking and His attitudes rub off on us when we spend time with Him in His Word and fellowship.

I had an opportunity to fall into comparison, but I recognized the familiar thinking and chose not to go into it. When I go into comparison, I also usually go into self-unacceptance and rejection. I was comparing myself with the other women that were around me on a weekend trip. The opportunity presented itself, but when I started to sense the oppression, I got up and walked around for a few minutes and realized, "This is comparison. Thank you very much, but I'm not taking it!" And I didn't!

I was very pleased that I recognized the mind trap of comparison just in time because when I allow this mind trap to take over my thinking, I go very low, very fast all the way into depression. But this time I caught it. When the Holy Spirit was teaching me about comparison, He told me that this was my besetting sin and I must keep a guard on my thinking in this area. If I did not, I could expect to find myself in self-unacceptance. This has been my pattern, but now I understand some of the suggestions that try to deceive me, and I am quicker to catch them. I have learned to recognize the first symptoms of this mind trap, and I can prevent myself from falling into it. It is just like knowing the first symptoms of a cold, the first signal that our bodies give us. If we can become aware of the oppression in our minds, at the onset of a mind trap, we can take measures to stop it in its tracks! Always turn to the Word immediately at the first thought of any oppression.

I do not know when comparison as a besetting sin (Hebrews 12:1–3) started in my life because it seems it has been there forever. After the self-unacceptance started with the division tables, I can remember I used to compare myself with how another little girl in school looked and dressed. Then I would look at all the other girls in the classroom and compare their dresses with what I had on. And I never quite measured up to them. I always felt beneath or inferior to them. That was where offense came in and trapped me. I always felt inferior to the other girls in my appearance, and I would get mad at everyone. Rejection came after the offense, and then I went into depression. I felt like a failure. I felt defeated. I wished I was not on the face of this earth anymore, and that meant I wished to die. Comparison and self-unacceptance took me all the way to depression and desiring death.

As an adult, sometimes I could catch the comparison and sometimes I could not. When I stayed in my mind, hashing something over for a few days, I knew I needed to do something to get control again in my spirit. When I started to learn about spiritual warfare, I realized that I could take the name of the mind trap, like comparison, and cast it out (2 Corinthians 10:3–6). I just got rid of it! I told it to go, in Jesus' Name. When I could not identify what displaced my spirit, I only had to remember that I am righteous (2 Corinthians 5:21) and every work of the enemy has been brought to nothing. As far as God is concerned, I am still the healed and the delivered. Today, I can think I am in a pit that I put myself into or I can have the thinking of God that says I am already delivered. It is my choice where I want to be. Since my emotions follow my thinking, it is a better place to think I am healed and delivered.

Psalm 51:12 says, *"Restore unto me the joy of Thy salvation and uphold me with Thy free spirit."* In the *New International Version* this same verse says, *"Restore to me the joy of Your salvation and grant me a willing spirit to sustain me."* We must recognize that no matter what deception comes at us or what thinking we are dealing with, we are already restored. We walk in a place of salvation, and we have a willing spirit that is ready to sustain us.

Psalm 111:9 says, *"He sent redemption unto his people: he hath commanded his covenant for ever: holy and revered is his name."* He sent redemption to us. We are His people and His work has not stopped. It is here for us to appropriate and walk in. Salvation is here for us. And it is not just the one-time experience of salvation when we are born again, but it is salvation from our soulish thinking patterns, besetting sins, and mind traps.

Joel 2:25 says: *"And I will restore to you the years that the locust hath eaten, the cankerworm and the caterpillar and the palmer worm, my great army which I sent among you."*

This is a good verse to remember when the devil is telling us that we have lack in some area of our lives. We can say, "Thank you, Father, whatever the locust or cankerworm or caterpillar has eaten, You will restore. The end result is that I am already restored now in my spirit." It is a decision that we make based on righteousness, which goes back to the love of God. It goes back to our relationship with God because God so loved us that He gave His Son and we entered into His righteousness. He covered us with His righteousness. Based on this fact we are already restored. This needs to be in the front of our thinking. This needs to be our understanding and our attitude. It does not matter what it looks like in the natural, we must take on God's thinking in our circumstances, and God said, "We are restored."

Romans 3:24 says, *"Being justified freely by his grace through the redemption that is in Christ Jesus . . ."* We are justified now by His grace. Nothing we could ever do could bring us into this position. It is all by Jesus Christ and His work on the cross for us.

First Corinthians 1:30 says, *"But of him are ye in Christ Jesus, who of God is made unto us wisdom, and righteousness, and sanctification, and redemption."* Jesus is made unto us wisdom, righteousness, sanctification, and redemption. This is part of our inheritance, and we can appropriate it today. We are in Jesus, and we have all these things now.

Second Corinthians 4:4 says: *"In whom the god of this world hath blinded the minds of them which believe not, lest the light of the glorious gospel of Christ, who is the image of God, should shine unto them."*

Satan is blinding the minds of people so that they will not believe the gospel of Christ. But he blinds the minds of both non-Christians and Christians. He blinds anyone who is in unbelief in an area of their souls. Satan blinds their minds so the light of the glorious gospel of Christ cannot be seen by them. I think it is important to remember that Jesus is the image of God. When we are dealing with Jesus, we are dealing with God the Father, as well as with the Holy Spirit. Spirit means "the essence of." So when we are dealing with the Holy Spirit, He is the essence of the totality of both God the Father and Jesus the Son.

Second Corinthians 4:6 says*: "For God, who commanded the light to shine out of darkness, hath shined in our hearts, to give the light of the knowledge of the glory of God in the face of Jesus Christ."*

Even though the god of this world blinds the minds of them that believe not, God has commanded the light to shine out of the darkness. The darkness is in our soul. When we have darkness in our souls, there is always a light that is commanded to shine on it. The light is in our spirits. The whole point is to get out of our double-mindedness and have the fullness of light come from our spirits out into your souls. Then it can come from our souls out to those around us.

We can believe and receive that the light God has commanded to shine in someone's mind and heart will be seen by them, even though at the moment they are blinded by Satan. God has commanded it to be seen, and so it will be seen. We can pray for laborers to come to these people so they may hear and understand and believe.

Acts 26:18 says:

"To open their eyes, and to turn them from darkness to light, and from the power of Satan unto God, that they may receive forgiveness of sins and inheritance among them which are sanctified by faith that is in me."

This is a wonderful Scripture to pray and to help hold our minds when someone's life looks hopeless and beyond repair. We can pray this verse for them as an act of intercession stating that sin has no hold on their lives now.

Romans 6:13–14 says:

"Neither yield your members as instruments of unrighteousness unto sin, but yield yourselves unto God as those alive from the dead and your members as instruments of righteousness unto God. For sin shall not have dominion over you for you are not under the law but under grace."

Victory over all mind traps has been bought and paid for by Jesus. His program of restoration is promised to us. Sometimes we find ourselves in a place where we recognize that we have yielded to wrong thinking. When we open our mind to *expectation*, for example, we have yielded our souls to be occupied by some of this wrong thinking. *Expectation* does not have the authority to dominate us unless we give it the opportunity. There is a progression in spiritual things that we need to be aware of. The first time we open our souls to *expectation*, some of our wills is taken captive. The next time we do, a little more of our wills is taken; until over a period of years, our wills are completely controlled by the mind trap of expectation. It becomes a familiar pattern of thinking for us.

This is why it is easy to say, "That's just me!" Why identify ourselves with thinking contrary to God? When we identify with the thinking of God, it releases our wills from the bondage of the mind traps. I once heard this statement: *"When practically applied, truth will give possibilities for faith and it will be releasing and uplifting. If it is not truth, when practically applied, it will bring heaviness, bondage, and have no possibilities for faith."* No matter what type of thinking has deceived us, these mind traps have no dominion over us. We are on the road to recovery the moment we decide to get out. The mind traps cannot keep us on the road to rejection and depression against our wills once we have decided to get out.

First John 3:19–20 says: *"And hereby we know that we are of the truth, and shall assure our hearts before him. For if our heart condemns us, God is greater than our heart, and knoweth all things."*

When we see a mind trap that has been a stronghold in our lives for a long time, we can go to God and do not have to stay condemned because He is bigger than our hearts. We have all been overtaken in certain areas. I can write about these mind traps because I have been highly developed in some of them and have experienced all of them. The patterns of thinking are the same no matter who the person is, and receiving the spiritual understanding is the first step to recovery. The next step is to make the decision to not allow the wrong thinking to take us down the road of rejection and depression again. This is my prayer:

> "Father, I repent and ask Your forgiveness for allowing the devil to influence my thinking and will. I thank You that the devil has no dominion over me. I thank You that You are bigger than my heart and know all things. I cast out comparison, offence, rejection and depression, and I receive all patterns of thinking exposed to me. I thank You, my mind and will are now loosed from any

control of the devil. I receive Your peace to flood
my mind and heart. In Jesus' Name. Amen."

It is important to let the Holy Spirit search our hearts to see what needs to be dealt with and taken authority over. The number of mind traps we have and the degree of entrapment all depends on how long we have been entertaining each one.

Philippians 2:9–11 says:

> *"Wherefore God also hath highly exalted him, and given him a name which is above every name: that at the name of Jesus every knee should bow, of things in heaven, and things in earth, and things under the earth; and that every tongue should confess that Jesus Christ is Lord, to the glory of God the Father."*

Everything has a name, and Jesus' Name is above every name in heaven, on the earth, and even under the earth. Be assured, when we cast something out, it has to go. Once we have cast out the mind trap, the Holy Spirit will continue to teach us. These are mental habits that we are now going to change. We have to realize we can still end up in depression many more times before we catch it and have complete control over it. Repent and back out. In the process, the Holy Spirit will teach us the specific *wile* that we missed. Next, we will find ourselves in rejection. When we see it, repent and back out. Again, the Holy Spirit will teach us how we got there.

Then there will come a day when we will hear the mind trap before it beguiles us, and when we speak the name of Jesus to it, it will leave. The more we practice this, the better we will get at it. This is when we arrive at the stage of maintenance. When we get to this place, it means we can look forward to a life free of depression. This means we have minds that are in subjection to our spirits. This process may take a few times or it may take weeks or months, depending on how established the pattern of thinking has become in our minds and how much our wills have been taken over by it.

We need to continue to fill ourselves up with God's Word, His peace, His love, and go on. Remember we are on a learning curve, and we have to understand how the wrong thinking is overtaking and controlling us, spiritually. It is a spiritual power play. The Holy Spirit will remind us of our decision not to allow the world's way of thinking to take up residence in our souls because that is what happens when we take a mind trap. The goal is to recognize the first signs and hear the mind trap before it enters our minds. When we arrive at this point, then Matthew 13:16 is fulfilled in our lives: *"But blessed are your eyes, for they see: and your ears, for they hear."*

The patterns of thinking that have become strongholds have been with us for many years. We are so well established in them that they are automatic habits. Even though we cast out the mind traps of offense, rejection, and depression, it will take time to see and hear all the different wiles the enemy has used to cement the particular mind trap for us. Be assured, however, that they have no dominion and cannot keep us in a defeated place. *But to overcome the mind trap will take diligence and plain hard work.* The hard work will mean practicing the Word and God's thinking instead of falling into our natural flesh reactions. When we make a quality decision to defeat wrongful thinking, we will do the work and we will change. We have to ask ourselves, "How bad do I want out?"

The only way to live is with our spirit-man in control of our souls. And it is the only way God wants us to live. First John 5:18 says: *"We know that whosoever is born of God sins not, but he that is begotten of God keeps himself and that wicked one touches him not."*

This is what it means to overcome. This is what it means to live this verse: *"Thy kingdom come, Thy will be done, on earth, as it is in heaven."* When we learn to keep ourselves away from the entrapment of the mind traps, the wicked one will not be able to touch us with them.

We are to continue to maintain our souls free from these mind traps, and there is a way of doing this. There are several Scriptures we want established in our minds:

Psalm 36:10: *"O continue thy loving-kindness unto them that know thee; and thy righteousness to the upright in heart."* We have to know that God has loving-kindness toward us, and His righteousness is always there. He is never going to take it away from us because He has made us righteous in His sight. We are the ones that stand back from it. It is always available for us in our thinking.

Psalm 102:28: *"The children of thy servants shall continue, and their seed shall be established before thee."* This verse is an encouragement for us as parents. Our seed will be established before God. He will continue to honor the covenant He has made with us and our children. Our children will not be forgotten. God promises that we have already been restored and already have everything that we will ever need to maintain what has been given to us.

Isaiah 61:7 is a very personal Scripture to us: *"For your shame you shall have double; and for confusion they shall rejoice in their portion: therefore, in their land they shall possess the double; everlasting joy shall be unto them."*

This promise of the double portion was given to us by the Holy Spirit through a man on TV one night. Dennis and I both received it together that night. It was given again to me by the Holy Spirit when He spoke to my heart to stretch our faith to apply this verse to every area of our lives. It was also spoken over us by a prophet in our church when we became elders. We heard this verse promised to us three times. This is why Isaiah 61:7 is such a personal and meaningful Scripture to us even today.

John 15:9 says, *"As the Father hath loved me, so have I loved you: continue ye in my love."* Part of maintaining is to make the choice that we are going to continue in God's love. We need to replace our selfish wills with God's love. Our thoughts and actions will give place to the love of God in our spirits. We will let Him have His way in us. This is why it is so important to be spirit-ruled.

Romans 11:22 says: *"Behold therefore the goodness and severity of God: on them which fell, severity; but toward thee, goodness, if thou continue in his goodness: otherwise thou also shalt be cut off."*

Again, this is a choice that we make. Either we walk in the blessings or we walk in the curses. God does not force anything on us. It is our choice. We are the ones who pull back. We are the ones who go astray. We can either walk in the goodness of God or in the severity of God. There is a judgment side of God. The judgment of God is already here as is His salvation. This means that if we decide to walk in the curses, we are going to be on the judgment side of God.

The devil was already judged when he was kicked out of heaven, but he has not yet reached nor experienced the fullness of his penalty. But he is already judged. If we take the devil's attitudes, we are going to be under the same judgment that he is under. Whatever condemnation the devil has already received the judgment we end up sharing with him. If we choose to be the child of the devil by taking his thinking, then we will walk in the fruit of it. The same is true of our words. They have the power of life or death in them. Proverbs 18:21 says, "Those that abide in them will eat the fruit of it." It is the whole process of sowing and reaping. We either choose life or we choose death. This goes on constantly, every day of our lives.

It says in Colossians 1:23:

> *"If ye continue in the faith grounded and settled, and be not moved away from the hope of the gospel, which ye have heard, and which was preached to every creature which is under heaven; whereof I Paul am made a minister."*

We have to choose to continue in the faith, being grounded and settled and not be moved away from the hope of the Gospel. This is how we are to maintain ourselves. We cannot let the devil steal the Word of God from us. If we allow his stealing of the Word, he will kill our hopes.

First Timothy 4:16 says: *"Take heed unto thyself, and unto the doctrine; continue in them; for in doing this thou shalt both save thyself, and them that hear thee."*

We must choose to take heed to ourselves and to the Word of God. I do not think we realize all the people our lives touch. People are watching us all the time to see what we do and what we say. They are watching our reactions. God is light, and Jesus is in the light. We need to choose to be like Jesus. We need to imitate what we see in the Word, and we need to react how Jesus would react.

First John 1:5 says, *"This then is the message which we have heard of him, and declare unto you, that God is light, and in him is no darkness at all."* God is light, and we have God, but we also have Jesus, who also is light. When we are maintaining, we are filling ourselves so full of God's Word that we will be full of light. When we are full of light, the darkness will have to flee. It is the same as when we sing praises. He inhabits our praises and the devil has to flee.

John 1:4–5 says, *"In Him was life; and the life was the light of men. And the light shineth in darkness; and the darkness comprehended it not."*

John 12:46 says, *"I am come a light into the world, that whosoever believeth on me should not abide in darkness."*

Jesus is still in the world because He is in us. He is the light to us first, and then He is the light to the world through us. People should be able to see His light in us. And sometimes when they do they might feel uncomfortable around us. The light will expose their darkness. They will not feel comfortable telling dirty jokes in front of us.

John 8:12 says: *"Then spoke Jesus again unto them, saying, I am the light of the world: he that followeth me shall not walk in darkness, but shall have the light of life."*

Many times I pray by receiving that the light and life of God would be seen by someone. I receive they would walk in the light. I receive for laborers to bring the light and the life of God to them. If they see this light, they will not be able to resist because they will be in the presence of God and experience the love of God. The hearts the Holy Spirit has prepared will receive the light, in Jesus' name.

Matthew 6:22–23 says:

> *"The light of the body is the eye: if therefore thine eye be single; thy whole body shall be full of light. But if thine eye be evil, thy whole body shall be full of darkness. If therefore the light that is in thee be darkness, how great is that darkness."*

I use this Scripture to remind myself of the singleness of purpose I am to live. I have to be single in my spirit and in my soul. This means no double-mindedness. We want the light to come out of our spirits and flood our souls. In order for the light within us to come up into our souls, we have to be in line with our spirits. We cannot be having one thinking in our spirits and another thinking in our souls. We have to have a singleness of purpose coming out of our spirits through our souls in order for our faith to work properly.

Faith works by knowledge. When we have knowledge of a promise from God's Word, it gives us hope. A foundation of hope in our spirits will give words to our faith. When we speak faith-filled words into the atmosphere, they will change our situation and bring us answers. Jesus said, when addressing the matter of which foods were clean or unclean, that it was not what goes into a man that defiles him, but what comes out of a man is what defiles him. This is why we are to be single in our purpose so that the pure life that is in our spirits can come through our souls to minister to and refresh those around us.

Our hope must also be based on the love of God for faith to work. Knowing what I have received and not forgetting it keeps my faith working. As I declare my faith-filled words, they will keep me single in mind and purpose. I will not be taking in evil, and I am not going to be full of darkness because I am going to keep my singleness of purpose. So it is important to remember that we have to have this singleness about us, especially when we are going to pray. Everything about our prayer has to already be settled within us. Rambling flowery prayers are ineffective. We have to already have our souls settled and know that it is in line with our spirits and with the Word of God. We have to know that everything that we are going to ask for is God's will.

Acts 13:47 says, *"For so hath the Lord commanded us, saying, I have set thee to be a light of the Gentiles, that thou shouldest be for salvation unto the ends of the earth."*

We are still called to minister and be lights to those around us who are not saved. We have the ability to shine. We are to be instruments that God can use to reach them, but they have to be able to see the light. We have the ability with God's help to turn a life around and break the power of Satan in their lives.

Romans 13:12 says, *"The night is far spent, the day is at hand: let us therefore cast off the works of darkness, and let us put on the armor of light."* The armor of light must be like a shield or the breastplate of righteousness that we are to have in readiness, as it says in 2 Corinthians 10:4–6, to revenge all disobedience to the knowledge of God. We are exhorted to "cast off the works of darkness." We have to cast them off. Since we are children of the day and children of the light, we must cast off the works of darkness because the day is at hand. Our purpose is to put on the armor of light. Take it by choice. If we automatically keep ourselves in the light and keep ourselves where we are in the light, then the evil one cannot touch us. He will come and try to bring things to us, but when we are in the light, we will not take them from him.

When our attitudes continue in line with God's Word, then the enemy's thinking cannot bring confusion to our souls and grief to our hearts. It is by the attitudes in our minds and our reactions that we give the devil the place to take hold within us. He cannot influence our spirits unless we let him. He can only influence our spirits when we give him a place in our souls. We cannot allow the mind traps to be the vehicle that he uses to divide us. He is already defeated! We keep him in the place of being defeated in our lives.

1. What is the proper source of information for our thought process?

   _____

2. How do we define maintenance or maintaining our minds (thought process)?

   _____

3.   What is the program of transformation we need to take?

_____

4.   How do we accomplish this transformation?

_____

5.   How do we identify with God in our circumstances?

_____

6.   How do we defeat any deception in our minds?

_____

7.   What is a good verse to remember when the thought of lack is attacking?

_____

8.   What is a good Scripture to pray for others who are in darkness?

_____

9.   Can our will be taken over by wrongful thinking?

_____

10. How can we protect ourselves?

_____

11. Explain how we can take authority over wrong thinking in the middle of a mind trap?

   _____

12. What does it mean to be in maintenance in reference to mind traps?

   _____

13. What does it mean to overcome?

   _____

SUMMARY

As the Word of God promises, I wanted to live as "more than a conqueror." It took some time to renew my thinking but today, I am enjoying this reality. If I keep my mind free of mind traps, keep my commitment to not react out of offense and stay free of rejection and depressive thinking, I can live in freedom, victory and maintain my God-given authority over my life and circumstances. God is no respecter of persons so the same freedom is available to whosoever applies these principles. Freely I have received this instruction from the Holy Spirit, so freely I give it to you.

There is a full rest from God available to His children. Applying the principles in this book will teach you how to maintain the rest in your soul which will affect your whole life. I believe and receive with you the victory you have over mind traps, offense, rejection, and depression. Jesus bore all we would ever encounter in this life on the cross. You are redeemed and have the victory, in Jesus' name!

ABOUT THE AUTHOR

For over thirty-seven years, Judith has spoken at women's groups, retreats, seminars, and counseled women in the body of Christ. Judith's teachings come with practical insights, given by the Holy Spirit, on how to live in victory over offense, rejection, and depression. She openly shares personal experiences as well as biblical examples to reveal how mind traps can start a destructive pattern of thinking in anyone. As cofounder of One Accord Ministries, Judith currently resides in Mammoth Lakes, California, with her husband of over forty-eight years.

CPSIA information can be obtained
at www.ICGtesting.com
Printed in the USA
FSOW02n0124270717
36821FS